Beyond Factory Farming:

Corporate Hog Narns and the Threat to Public Health, the Environment, and Rural Communities

Edited by
Alexander M. Ervin
Cathy Holtslander
Darrin Qualman
Rick Sawa

Copyright © 2003

All rights reserved. No part of this book may be reproduced or transmitted in any form or by any means, electronic or mechanical, including photocopying, or by any information storage or retrieval system, without permission in writing from the publisher.

National Library of Canada Cataloguing in Publication

National Conference on Intensive Livestock Operations (2nd : 2002 : Saskatoon, Sask.)
Beyond factory farming / edited by Alexander Ervin ... [et al.].

Proceedings of 2nd Annual National Conference on Intensive Livestock Operations held Nov. 9, 2002 in Saskatoon, Sask.
Includes bibliographical references.
ISBN 0-88627-366-8

. Livestock factories—Congresses. 2. Livestock factories—Canada—Congresses. 3. Canada—Rural conditions—Congresses.
I. Ervin, Alexander M. (Alexander Mackay), 1942- II. Title.

SF391.3.N38 2002 338.1'76'00971 C2003-905031-9

Printed and bound in Canada

Published by

Canadian Centre for Policy Alternatives–Saskatchewan
2717 Wentz Ave., Saskatoon, SK S7K 4B6
Tel 306-978-5308 Fax 306-922-9162
http://www.policyalternatives.ca
ccpasask@sasktel.net

Contents

Acknowledgements

This book has been almost a year in the making. The authors presented their papers at the 2nd Annual National Conference on Intensive Livestock Operations entitled Beyond Factory Farming held in Saskatoon, Saskatchewan on November 9, 2002. The editors would like to thank the wide variety of organisations that sponsored and organized the conference and provided seed money for this publication: Global Resource Action Centre for the Environment (GRACE), the Grain Services Union, Saskatchewan Federation of Labour, Saskatchewan Union of Nurses, the Saskatchewan Office of the Canadian Centre for Policy Alternatives (CCPA), National Farmers Union, Saskatchewan Eco Network, Environmental Defence Canada, The Sierra Club of Canada, The Sierra Club of Canada-Saskatoon Parklands Group, The Sierra Club (U.S.), The Council of Canadians, Hog Watch Manitoba, the College of Arts and Sciences—University of Saskatchewan, the Department of Religious Studies and Anthropology—University of Saskatchewan, Oxfam Canada, and the Saskatchewan Environmental Society. The conference organising committee is deserving of recognition: Lisa Bechthold, Sandy Ervin, Loretta Gerlach, Cathy Holtslander, Larry Hubich, Glen Koroluk, Isabel Muzichuk, Simon Neufeld, Darrin Qualman, and Rick Sawa—conference coordinator. The editors are grateful to the National Office of the Canadian Centre for Policy Alternatives for its assistance with publishing this book.

About CCPA-Sask

The book you hold is the first book-length publication of the Saskatchewan Office of the Canadian Centre for Policy Alternatives (CCPA-Sask.). Nationally, the CCPA was launched in 1980 and works to promote research on economic and social issues facing Canada. Through its activities the CCPA wants to demonstrate that there are thoughtful alternatives to the limited perspective of business research institutes and many government agencies. To achieve its ends the CCPA publishes research reports, newsletters, and books; sponsors conferences; and organizes briefings.

CCPA-Sask. was launched in 2001 and is a non-partisan, non-profit research institute dedicated to producing and promoting progressive economic and social policy research of importance to Canadian and Saskatchewan citizens. To contact CCPA-Sask., call (306) 978-5308.

This book is partly based on a conference that CCPA-Sask. helped organize in 2002.

Introduction

Modern hog production does not merely mean more hogs in larger barns, any more than a Nike factory is a bunch of cobblers in one big building or a Wal-mart is just a bigger version of the old general store.

Hog mega-barns—also known as Intensive Livestock Operations (ILOs) or Confined Animal Feeding Operations (CAFOs)—are tightly linked to corporate packing plants and have completely transformed how hogs are produced: the ownership and control of the barns, their relationship to the communities in which they are located, the destination of profits, conditions of work; treatment of animals, the barns' impact on the environment, and the relation of local citizens to their government.

Part industrial revolution and part globalization, the shift towards factory farm hog production mirrors and drives larger changes in our communities and economies. The debate over hog production is part of the larger debate on globalization—the power of transnational corporations, the questions of who should own the economy, and who the economy should serve.

Vertical Integration

Today's hog mega-barns are linked—either through contracts or outright ownership—to transnational pork packers and food processors. Furthermore, these corporate packer/producers often own feed mills, grain collection facilities, and livestock sales yards. They characterize their approach as "barley to bacon" or "squeal to meal." They practice "vertical integration."

Vertical integration profoundly changes the economics of hog production in a way that is toxic to independent, family farm hog producers. While independent farmers need to make a profit on the hogs they raise and sell, vertically-integrated corporations are far less dependent on profits from hogs. For integrated producers, low hog prices mean lower profits from their barns but this is offset by the corresponding larger profits from their packing plants.

Vertically integrated packers take their own hogs first, so independent family farmers competing with them have difficulty gaining access to the market. Mega-barns are driving family farms out of the business, not because family farms cannot produce hogs as cheaply, but because, in an industry dominated by large sellers and buyers, small producers are often denied access to markets.

The Extraction of Wealth

When families produce hogs on farms they own, they receive the profits and they spend those profits in their communities. When corporations produce hogs, the profits—and management salaries—are extracted from the area, often to an urban financial centre.

Family farmers buy most of their supplies locally while large producers tend to bypass local stores and purchase supplies in large distant cities, threatening the survival of local businesses.

Corporate mega-barns—like corporate-owned retailers, restaurants, or services—channel the wealth away from the places in which it is produced. This extraction process usually leaves the wealth-producing area economically disadvantaged while concentrating money and power in the hands of a few in the dominant financial centres. This process is paralleled by a global extraction of wealth from developing countries to the world's dominant nations.

The Dumping of Wastes

While the industrial livestock system efficiently concentrates and moves the wealth out of the countryside, it concentrates wastes and deposits them in rural air, water, and soil. Each hog mega-barn creates millions of gallons of liquid manure slurry which is stored, then spread on the land, threatening groundwater aquifers as well as surface water bodies with its leaks, spills, or contaminated run-off. Excessive manuring can lead to problems with soil fertility. Barn ventilation and off-gassing from manure "lagoons" (more like open septic tanks) lead to health problems, exacerbate global warming, drive down property values, and drive away economic enterprises that require fresh air and pure water. The touted "efficiency" of factory farming is simply a matter of off-loading the costs of maintaining air, water, and soil quality onto the environment and neighbours.

The Transformation of Work

In the 1980s, many North Americans learned the word "entrepreneur." The impression given by the media was that more and more of us would be self-employed—prosperous masters of our own destinies. The opposite was occurring, however. Even as magazine covers touted the age of the entrepreneur, corporations were busy flushing local families out of the economy. Grocery stores, confectionaries, movie theatres, and restaurants, once owned by local families, were being snapped up by transnationals, either through direct ownership or through franchising.

Farming is the only major sector in the North American economy where the means of production is still owned by local families. The corporate and industrial restructuring of Canada's hog sector (and an identical restructuring of the U.S. poultry and dairy sectors) is just the latest stage in a corporate drive to displace local family ownership within our economy.

In 1991, there were nearly 30,000 Canadian farm families producing hogs. Ten years later, half were gone—pushed out by the industrialization of the sector. As corporations seize control of hog production from local families, the work of raising hogs is completely transformed: the people inside of the barns no longer own the hogs or control their work, their experience of quality of work life decreases, and their health risks multiply.

High levels of animal dander and fecal dust combined with high levels of ammonia can result in unsafe working conditions in hog barns. On a family farm, hog production is usually one part of a mixed operation. The farmer works in the barn for part of the day but he or she also works in the field growing crops and in the home office managing the business. In contrast, mega-barn employees work almost exclusively and for long hours inside the hog barn. This prolonged exposure to noise and polluted air greatly increases the potential for health damage.

Links to the Local Community

Just as the move from family farm to corporate ownership severs the links between the barns and the people working inside of them, so too does it sever the links between the barns and the people living in the community around them.

When hogs are raised on family farms, the family usually lives in the same yard as the hogs. The owners, who are also the workers, are intimately connected to the hogs and decisions about the hogs affect the family owners first. In contrast, corporate mega-barn owners live hundreds of miles away and even the workers usually live off-site.

When barns are corporate-owned, decisions that affect the barn or its community may be made thousands of miles away. Further, the expected life of the mega-barns is only 15 to 20 years. Unlike local families who have close, multi-generational links to their farms and communities, corporate owners' obligations are only to shareholders.

Perhaps the most distressing effect upon community members occurs when the entry of a mega-barn operation breaks bonds of friendship and drives a wedge of animosity between family members as conflict escalates between proponents and opponents of the industry. Experience shows that such tears in the social fabric are nearly impossible to mend.

The Hogs

Industrialization requires large-scale production, centralized control, and uniform and predictable products and inputs. The industrialization of the hog sector follows this model. While family farms are more able to adapt to diversity and unpredictability, industrial hog production demands predictability and the control of as many variables as possible. This need for control and uniformity is hard on the hogs.

In hog mega-barns, sows are caged in "farrowing crates." Never allowed outside the sealed barn, never allowed to socialize or to forage or dig in straw, the animals' lives must be restructured to accommodate the mass-production process.

Furthermore, hogs from the mega-barn are not the product themselves, but merely an input to an equally industrialized packing sector that also demands uniform and predictable inputs. This need has fostered keen interest in hog genetics and in "improved" hog rearing practices: the aim is to turn out hogs that are nearly identical in their uniformity. By producing increasingly uniform hogs, corporate packers/producers can lower the skill needed to work in packing plants and thus reduce the pay.

The Role of Government

In destroying family farm hog producers and industrializing pork production, governments have been the handmaidens to industry. Governments in Canada have dismantled farmers' single-desk marketing boards, weakened environmental laws, taken siting jurisdiction away from local governments, refused to grant worker protections, facilitated migrant workers, promoted—and even financed—mega-scale pork production. Governments have utterly compromised their legitimate role as servants of the citizens by entering into clear conflicts of interests—becoming the promoters, investors, owners, inspectors, regulators, and legislators in charge of the industry.

In lowering standards to attract corporate packer/producers, governments seem genuinely frightened—scared that, in the new global economy, powerful mobile capital will leave their community or province behind. In the new global economy, governments negotiate investment and trade agreements that limit governments' ability to legislate or regulate in the interests of their citizens. The result is a race to the bottom, where the "winner" is the one who can give away the most resources and give away the most control to corporations.

Organization of the Book

This book will take the reader through the broad setting of factory farming in Canada and the U.S. to the front lines where people are dealing with specific issues and locales.

Articles by Kendall Thu and John Ikerd present political economic outlooks that place the emergence of vertical integration and corporate farming in historical and economic perspective. Thu's anthropological approach shows us the ominous impact of factory farming in the context of globalization. He reminds us that regular and often devastating patterns of social change come from transitions in the ways that we produce food. Ikerd points to the recolonization of North America where farmers and communities are marginalized to interests far beyond their regions.

Next we move into case studies and details of ILO impacts. Fred Tait's article moves from the political economy into the story of Manitoba's hog industry transformation, where "single desk marketing" that helped level the field for independent hog farmers was eliminated, through to the building of the giant meat packing plant in Brandon.

Rick Dove presents devastating evidence from North Carolina where politicians in collusion with transnational corporations brought about a chronic, state-wide, environmental and health disaster. Dove's tireless and generous work in reaching out and telling of North Carolina's experience provides a warning to Canadian activists as American jurisdictions create barriers to ILO expansion and corporations in turn seek out Canadian locations.

Next, Bill Weida, through examples from western U.S., shows that people have often been considered merely obstacles to be removed in order to make way for mega-barn development and expansion.

Biologist Bill Paton from Brandon University has prepared a comprehensive indictment of the biochemical impacts (especially odour) that will give community activists much ammunition for their resistance to intensive livestock operations.

Providing comic relief and clever reminders of negative consequences, Brian Storey gives us a song patterned on Dr. Seuss's "Green Eggs and Ham."

The next section focuses on action by citizens opposing factory farming. Lisa Bechthold tells the tale of her Alberta community's resistance to hog barn expansion. Her appendices provide practical models for community activists showing how to organize and mobilize community efforts.

An issue that has always bedevilled resistance is the rights of workers at hog barns. Through "right to farm legislation" corporate interests have been able to bypass fair labour standards. Larry Hubich's work with the Saskatchewan Grain Services Union led to the unionization of workers at a Saskatchewan hog barn.

Simon Neufeld and Miné Elbi, working through Toronto-based Environmental Defence Canada, document two case studies in Canadian communities where legal action has been used to stem intensive livestock operation expansion.

Finally we return to political economic perspectives with Roger Epp's chapter focusing on the Canadian context, which calls for action and respect for rural Canadians who for decades have suffered the onslaught of actions and interests beyond their communities.

Conclusion

The agricultural transition from family farm production to factory farm production is both a microcosm and a major strategy of globalization, as corporations seek ever-increasing economic and political power. The corporate assault on our economy, our cultures, and political autonomy is multi-faceted and widespread. Likewise, the broad-based citizen resistance to intensive livestock production is part of the world-wide resistance to globalization. Understanding the corporate takeover of hog production can provide us with a base from which to develop policy alternatives for livestock production, and agriculture in general.

The vision for rural Canada's future needs to embrace humane livestock production that supports the well-being of communities, farmers, workers, and ecosystems while providing high-quality, wholesome food to consumers. This book illustrates that corporate industrial livestock production is not an inevitable outcome of "progress" but an element of a political agenda being pursued by a corporate and government power structure. There are alternatives, and we can go *Beyond Factory Farming.*

Chapter 1
Industrial Agriculture, Democracy, and the Future
by Kendall Thu

The lesson of human social and political evolution suggests that the current global concentration of agricultural production, processing, and distribution into fewer hands portends a future of increasing human struggle and conflict. From the hunting and gathering !Kung Bushmen of the Kalahari Desert, to the horticultural Tsembaga of New Guinea, to the intensive agricultural Maya and Aztec civilizations, to the aristocratic estates and slaves of the American South, to the feudal landholders of Western Europe, to the highly industrialized hog production and processing factories in Canada and the U.S., all illustrate the anthropological lesson that the ways food is gathered, grown, and distributed fundamentally shape human societies. Through the prehistoric, historic, and contemporary record of human adaptation, a reasonably clear pattern is discernible—as the food system becomes more centralized, so too do political, economic, and even religious systems. Indeed, the current rapid centralization of ownership and control over land and food does not necessarily free the remainder of society from tilling the soil to pursue affluence, but rather alienates and oppresses a society's inhabitants.

Over the past century, the global shift to an industrialized form of agriculture is arguably as important for our world order as the emergence of agriculture itself some 10,000 years ago. The advent of domesticated animals and plants brought with it profound changes in human adaptation, namely the rise of cities, nation-states, the emergence of centralized political power, differences between classes of people, full-time conscripted armies, taxation, and many other characteristics resulting in a dramatic departure from our hunting and gathering past. The contemporary shift to a global industrial model of food production and distribution reveals equally compelling consequences for human adaptation.

As anthropologists know, all societies are formatively shaped by a food production and distribution infrastructure that is essential to their survival. In the past, local or regional systems of food production and exchange shaped individual societies in terms of their social organizations, economic systems, and political structures. As the shift from production for one's own consumption gave way to production for market exchange, the production of agricultural surplus no longer meant feeding a society's inhabitants, but rather it allowed political control over the distribution of a basic resource to serve other interests, such as enhancing wealth. Yet, this type of centralization was largely local or regional—even the expansive Roman, Ottoman, or Viking empires were regional in scope largely because each entailed the notion of political expansion from one area to another. Today's globalization process may be much different. With the centralization of agriculture in all areas of the globe an agricultural infrastructure is present that allows for a global centralization of food production and distribution by multinational corporations not bound by traditional nation-states. In other words, today's centralized global political order may not be the result of political domination by one nation-state-based empire over another, but rather a more insidious centralized world order emergent from a common centralized agricultural infrastructure controlled by non-state entities. This emergent power wrests control of land and resources from local inhabitants and is notably present with the emergence of industrialized livestock production.

Ask neighbours of an industrial hog operation in rural Saskatchewan or North Carolina about their experiences. In vivid detail they will describe their diminished quality of life, the impairment of surface and groundwater, the horrific odour, the social upheaval and divisions among neighbours, friends, and family members, the displacement of family farmers and rural decay, the inequitable burden placed on impoverished rural neighbourhoods and communities of colour, concerns over health problems from airborne emissions, intimidation by local officials and industry representatives, and the collusion between industry, government, and research institutions. Each of these areas is in itself worthy of attention. Taken together, they paint a compelling picture of a fundamental pathology undermining the core infrastructure of society. I argue that without addressing the inequities and imbalances in our food systems, any hope of real social and political equity, as well as environmental stewardship, are likely impossible for any society.

Here I examine the scope of problems resulting from the industrialization of agriculture, with particular attention to the livestock sector in North America. Invoking an anthropological framework, I suggest that the common inability of local, rural communities in Canada and the U.S. to find adequate redress to known and emerging problems of factory livestock operations is a consequence of a more fundamental problem of concentrated political power that is an outgrowth of highly centralized food systems. Consequently, factory livestock operations and the industrial food system of which they are a part are not a concern just of farmers and rural communities, but are of fundamental importance to all members of a society that value democracy.

Industrialized Food and Global "De-Agriculturalization"

Industrialized agriculture refers to a system of food production and distribution dependent on fossil fuel inputs such as fertilizers, pesticides, machinery, and gasoline (Barlett, 1989; Thu & Durrenberger, 1998). It is also characterized by the replacement of labour (farmers) with capital-intensive production and distribution technology for mass production. The industrialization of agriculture is viewed by some, lauded by others, as a natural model of economic growth and efficiency. A standard economic view of the industrialization of food production is that it is yet another example of industry maturation through achievement of economies of scale. However, broader empirical examinations of industrialized agriculture have revealed a large constellation of economic costs (externalities) frequently ignored by economists who tend to focus on a narrow range of variables to interpret efficiency and economies of scale (Durrenberger & Thu, 1996; Thu & Durrenberger, 1998; Thu et al., 1996). The rapid emergence of environmental and public health costs of industrialized agriculture, particularly in the livestock sector, have revealed the myopia of traditional economic analyses.

Industrialized agriculture has contributed significantly to a profound systemic change in how our world population lives and sustains itself, namely the global movement away from agriculture. In 1950 almost two-thirds of the world's population was principally engaged in agricultural activities. A mere 50 years later this figure was reduced to 40% (see Figure 1). The staggering numbers of peoples involved, the speed of change, and the social and cultural consequences of this metamorphosis reflect a vital change in our world order. According to projections contained in a joint report prepared by the United Nations, the International Labour Organization, and the Food and Agriculture Organization of the United Nations, the year 2025 will witness a world with less than one-third of its inhabitants engaged in primary production. If this prediction rings true, it means that in the 75-year period from 1950 to 2025 the number of people in the world engaged in agriculture will have been reduced by more than half. These changes, occurring within a single generation, may be as dramatic and far-reaching for the human world order as any change since the emergence of agriculture itself.

Figure 1. Percentage of World Population in Production Agriculture

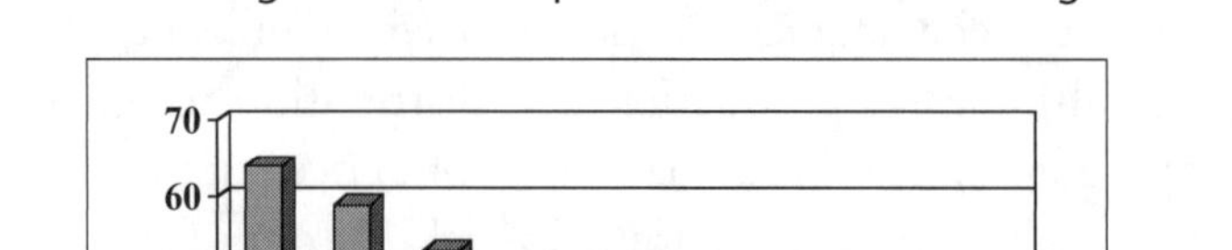

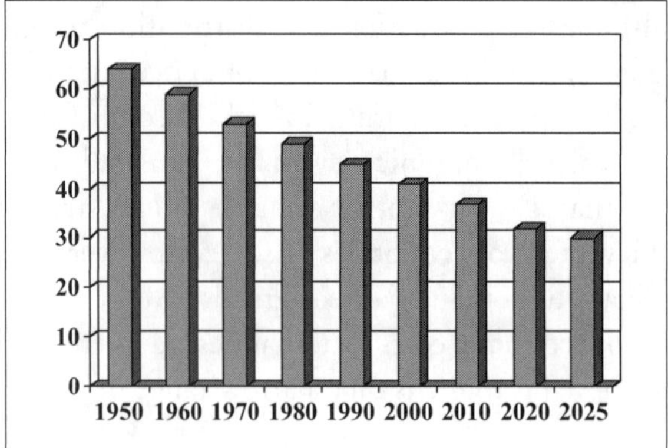

An examination of select United Nations' statistics reveals that this pattern of agricultural decline is indeed global, cross-cutting geographical and political borders. A division of the world into "developed" and "less developed" regions reveals a similar pattern at different stages (see Figure 2). More industrialized regions of the world reflect a process of agricultural change that has seemingly run its course, with only 8% of their combined populations engaged in primary production by 1990. This means that in a 40-year period 28% of the total population in developed regions has moved away from primary production as its principle means of subsistence. Projections for the year 2025 indicate a further reduction of this agricultural population to approximately 2%.

So-called less developed regions reflect a similar pattern of agricultural change, though at a slightly slower pace. While the general pattern is the same, less developed regions have a much higher percentage of their population still in primary production. In 1990 fully 56% of the combined populations in less developed nations engaged in some form of agriculture as their primary source of subsistence versus only 8% in developed areas. However, projections up through the year 2025 reveal a continuation of the pattern of declining agricultural populations in less-developed regions. Unless dramatic world changes are forthcoming, it seems reasonable to simply add the 75-

Figure 2. Global Comparison of Declines in Agricultural Populations Between Developed and Underdeveloped States

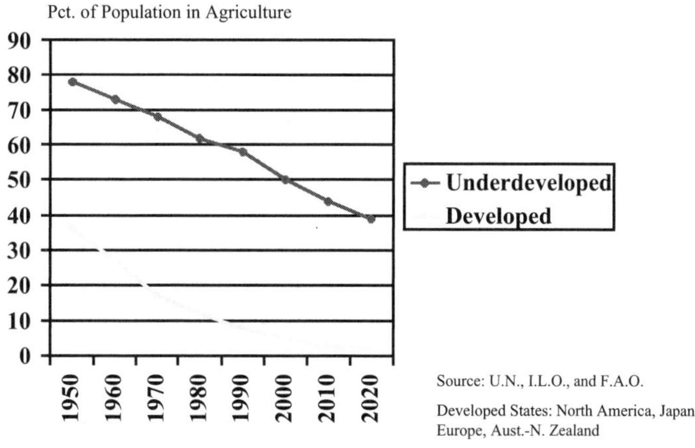

year curve for developed regions onto the end of the 75-year curve for less developed regions. This provides a rough estimation of how a continuation of this pattern would appear in less developed regions another 75 years into the future.

The global decline in farmers parallels the inverse growth of multinational agribusinesses. For example, the largest privately held company in the United States is Cargill, which accounts for nearly half of the world's global grains. Cargill has 97,000 employees spanning 59 countries as part of its nearly 51 billion-dollar annual business. Other global food giants include the likes of Nestlé, Kraft, and ConAgra, which collectively constitute a trillion-dollar industry, second only to the pharmaceutical industry as the largest in the U.S. As farmers disappear and on-farm profit margins narrow or are non-existent, profits for global food conglomerates soar. For example, Cargill's profits rose 131% in a mere one-year period between 2001 and 2002.

The global pattern of agricultural industrialization and increasingly centralized control is exemplified in North American agriculture, particularly the livestock industry in recent years. The swine industry is a classic example of this industrialization process. There is very little difference between the total U.S. inventory of hogs in the year 2000 (59.3 million) compared with the total inventory of hogs produced over 80 years earlier in 1915 (60.6 million) (USDA-NASS, n.d.). While overall production volume has changed little, the structure of the industry has shifted radically. As revealed in Figure 3, the number of hog producers in the U.S. declined precipitously from the 1960s to the present. Notable in this regard is the rapid rate of decline and concurrent emergence of relatively large production operations. For example, in a mere six-year period from 1993 to 1999, there was a 250% increase in the total U.S. hog inventory concentrated in operations with 5,000 or more hogs each (USDA-NASS, n.d.).

The pattern is similar in Canada where the last two decades (1981 to 2001) alone have witnessed the loss of over 60,000 farms, a 22% decline (Statistics Canada, n.d.). During the same period, over 40,000 farms have ceased raising hogs, a whopping 72% loss of hog produc-

Figure 3. Total U.S. Hog Farmers from 1965 to 1999 (USDA NASS)

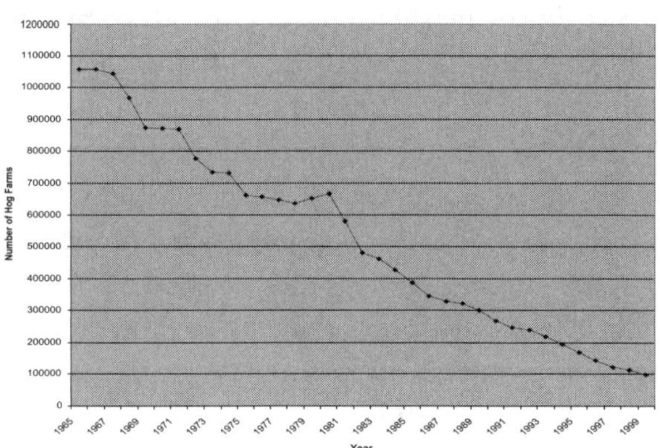

ers. Several Canadian provinces are experiencing the same dramatic disappearance of hog producers as large-scale factory hog operations become entrenched. For example, in Saskatchewan, the total volume of hogs produced nearly doubled between 1981 and 2001. At the same time, the number of farms producing hogs declined over 80%, from nearly 9,200 to 1,700.

This precipitous decline in farms has been well-documented by anthropologists and rural sociologists to have eroding social and economic consequences for rural areas. Rooted in the work of the anthropologist Walter Goldschmidt (1947), a whole generation of research (Thu et al., 1996) has demonstrated that it is simply better for the social and economic fabric of rural communities to have more farmers producing food than to have production concentrated in the hands of a few. The core of the problem, discovered by Goldschmidt over 50 years ago, is that, when farming is practised on a scale that exceeds a family's ability to provide the main source of labour and management, it tends to acquire industrial relations of production in which ownership and management are separated from labour. As a result, this industrialized form of agriculture tends to become disarticulated from surrounding communities, resulting in social inequities, poverty, and a range of attendant social, economic, and environmental pathologies. Indeed, the range of problems associated with industrialized hog production is particularly disconcerting.

The proliferation of industrial hog production facilities and the concentration of swine ownership into fewer hands parallel technological changes. The most notable is the shift from pasture-based and open-lot production to total animal confinement, beginning in the early 1970s. The shift to totally confined production does provide an advantage to hog producers in temperate regions by providing an antidote to harsh climatic conditions which impede growth rates and time to market. When hogs must expend a larger proportion of their nutrients in the form of energy to protect them from the cold, their feed-to-meat conversion rates decline. In addition, enclosed production units provide an opportunity for stricter control of feed rationing and reproduction. However, the costs of confined animal feeding operations, particularly as they take on characteristics of industrial-scale production, are dramatic.

In addition to the economic costs for rural areas, a wide variety of environmental and public health problems have emerged as a result of the industrialization of livestock production (Iowa State University and the University of Iowa Study Group, 2002). Surface and groundwater contamination occurs from the huge volumes of manure produced. In contrast to the solid manure produced in open-air hog production, confined animal production means the storage and management of manure in a liquid form that is much more mobile. Swine produce over twice as much manure per day compared with humans, and the biological oxygen demand (BOD) of undiluted hog waste is 160 times greater than raw human municipal sewage. In addition, the huge volumes of antibiotics fed livestock, primarily served up as growth promotants in feed, are largely excreted in the liquid manure. Consequently, antibiotics, as well as antibiotic-resistant bacteria, join the nitrogen, phosphorous, heavy metals, and other swine manure constituents that find their way into, and degrade, surface and ground waters. Indeed, the problem has become so pronounced in the U.S. that the Environmental Protection Agency (EPA) was legally required to develop new regulations to issue discharge permits for large-scale animal production facilities comparable to the types of permits typically issued to urban factories.

In revisions to the Federal Clean Water Act originally promulgated in 1972, new rules concerning livestock operations were issued in December 2002. These rules specify the primary problem as coming from large livestock operations, in part because large operations are more likely than smaller operations to have an insufficient land base for utilizing manure nutrients. In short, an imbalance has been created in which the nutrients required to grow hogs are taken from local farm environments and concentrated in small areas. As a result, solid manure that was once widely distributed fertilizer for large numbers of sustainable farm systems is transformed into a liquid industrial waste product contaminating the water and air.

A common environmental problem created by large concentrations of hogs and manure is the degradation of air quality. Some 160 volatile organic compounds are emitted from liquid hog manure and their odiferous character can offend even the most seasoned farmer or rural resident. Industrial production facilities housing thousands of swine come with storage facilities holding hundreds of thousands, even millions, of gallons of liquid manure. Large exhaust fans dot the exterior walls of these facilities testifying to the fact that the interior ambient environment is not particularly healthy, so particulates and gases are forced outside. Indeed, fully a third of workers working inside these facilities will develop one or more chronic respiratory problem in direct response to exposure to gas and dust mixtures (Merchant et al., 2002). Compounds such as hydrogen sulfide and ammonia, blended with dusts and endotoxin, also create problems for neighbours, particularly when large volumes of manure are stored in liquid form. Anyone who has spent even a little time on farms clearly understands that some type of odour is inherent to the agricultural environment. However, concentrating hundreds of thousands of gallons of liquid manure in one area is anything but natural and can have a devastating quality-of-life effect on neighbouring farmers and other rural residents.

More than merely an unpleasant sensation, odour can have life-altering consequences for denizens of rural communities who relish a way of life premised on enjoying the out-of-doors (Thu & Durrenberger, 1994; Flora et al., 2002). Neighbours of industrial swine production operations frequently share common views, values, expectations, and experiences concerning country living. Their lives revolve around centrally cherished life values consisting of family, friends, home, and faith. The ability to express these values through activities at their homes is centrally important to their quality of life. Their homes and property are their primary universe and as such the principal arena in which they experience and express their core values concerning family and friends. The encroachment of a factory livestock facility near their homes and their properties is significantly disruptive of numerous individual activities and expectations of rural living. Moreover, it affects the most sacrosanct areas inherently important for their quality of life. The freedom and independence associated with life oriented toward outdoor living gives way to a sense of violation and infringement as activities associated with central dimensions of their lives are taken away. Children and grandchildren cannot experience the unfettered joy of outdoor life in the country—jumping on the trampoline, bicycling, playing in the pool, picking flowers and playing with bugs in the yard, and inviting friends over to play. Additionally, parents become upset when their children are affected by odours, which in turn has a ripple effect creating frustration, anger, and family tensions.

Social occasions when family and friends come together are affected either in actual practice or through disruption of plans or routines that normally provide social cohesion and a sense of neighbourhood belonging—backyard barbecues, visits by friends and family. Their homes are no longer an extension of, nor a means for, enjoying the outdoors. Rather, their homes become a barrier against the outdoors that harbour intrusive odours. In short, the odour significantly infringes on their ability to enjoy their home, property, family, and lives. Their homes and property are intimately connected to their ability to express, appreciate, and enjoy centrally important values in their lives involving family, friends, and home. As such, the odour disrupts more than an itemized list of activities on a calendar; it takes away the most basic elements of their lives and offers them no control in return.

Recent public health research has shown that neighbours of large-scale swine operations are also at elevated risk for health problems (Merchant et al., 2002; Thu, 2002). In addition to odour malfeasance, neighbours appear to be experiencing elevated rates of health symptoms related to the upper respiratory tract. Symptoms such as excess coughing, wheezing, chest tightness, dizziness, and shortness of breath appear more frequently among neighbours of large-scale swine operations when compared with other groups in rural areas. Indeed, results indicate neighbours may be experiencing clusters of symptoms similar to the well-documented toxic or inflammatory respiratory effects among interior workers.

With the mounting evidence of negative social, economic, environmental, and public health consequences of industrial scale livestock production, the natural question is "why?" Why not simply approach our government representatives, explain the problem by showing them the scientific research coupled with local experiences of neighbours, and have them make changes? After all, representative democratic free governments are supposed to exist to protect individual rights and ensure the public interest is being served. Despite the litany of problems associated with industrialized agriculture, the most fundamental issue is not the air, water, or even the decay of rural communities. Most problematic is the fundamental erosion of freedom and democracy via the centralization of political power that follows from industry consolidation. How can we fix water quality, air quality, economic decay, rural community social upheaval, and rural health, if we lose our freedom of speech and find a tightening noose around channels of access to government, scientific research, and the courts? Indeed, deeply disturbing efforts to thwart independent agricultural research, muzzle public criticism of industrial livestock facilities, and force independent family farmers to pay the government for messages about their occupation that they do not agree with signal tendencies not of freedom and democracy, but of autocracy and authoritarianism.

Democracy, Farming, and the Future

In 1996, famed U.S. talk show host Oprah Winfrey brought vegetarian activist Howard Lyman on her show to discuss Mad Cow Disease and the livestock industry. The show's content suggested the possibility that Mad Cow Disease could spread from cows to humans. To audience applause, an effervescent Oprah proclaimed that "It has just stopped me from eating another burger!" What Oprah probably thought was just another show, another day at the office, turned out to be a major legal battle brought against her by the Texas cattle industry. The Texas cattlemen contended that Oprah and her guests spoke disparagingly about beef which had a significant effect on consumer confidence resulting in considerable financial losses for the industry. No doubt Oprah was unaware that Texas, similar to 12 other U.S. states, had passed "veggie libel laws" which prohibit people from speaking disparagingly about agriculture. A representative example can be seen in South Dakota's law which defines disparagement as follows:

> Disparagement: *dissemination in any manner* to the public of any information that implies that an agricultural food product is not safe for consumption by the public or that generally accepted agricultural and management practices make agricultural food products unsafe for consumption by the public. (South Dakota, Title 20, Chapter 20-10A, n.d.)

What may seem an innocuous and inconspicuous law actually represents a bold frontal attack on the fundamental core of the First Amendment of the U.S. Constitution, namely freedom of speech. U.S. citizens in these states are supposed to shut up and not talk publicly about food safety and accept the state's proposition that there are "generally accepted agricultural and management practices" that will protect them. Aside from the glaringly obvious constitutional question, who gets to decide what constitutes "generally accepted agricultural and management practices?" I have a hunch neighbours of industrial scale livestock operations would not be the first line of industry experts outlining what is "generally accepted."

In and of themselves, veggie libel laws are reason for concern. Unfortunately, they are not an isolated event, but rather part of an emerging pattern of attempts to curtail free speech over problems of industrialized agriculture. For example, in 2002 agricultural industry lobbyists in Illinois tried to get the state legislature to illegalize attempts to photograph confined animal production facilities. This was an effort to respond to images produced by animal welfare groups showing deplorable living conditions for livestock. Just recently in 2003, the agricultural industry in Minnesota passed an amendment to an organic transition cost-share bill that would blacklist groups who have "taken action" to prevent some type of agricultural activity:

> The commissioner may not provide a grant to or contract with an individual or organization that in the previous 36 months has taken, or participated financially in, an action to prevent a person from engaging in agricultural activities or expanding an agricultural operation. (Minnesota State Legislature, 2003)

Similar problems appear in Canada. In the discussion aftermath of the Industrial Livestock Conference sponsored by the Canadian Centre for Policy Alternatives, rural residents asked how they could speak out against industrial livestock operations without facing the prospect of "slap lawsuits."

Other more insidious forms of suppression are also evident. For example, Utah is home to possibly the largest hog operation in the world. The state is also the home of the Church of Latter Day Saints known as the Mormons. When a partnership of large agribusiness interests built Circle 4 Farms near the little town of Milford in southern Utah, they involved the Mormon Church in their efforts by hiring Church bishops in their management team. Local residents who began airing concerns over a 50,000-sow operation and manure lagoons the size of football fields, were faced with social pressure and the possible stigma of not just going against an agribusiness interest, but by extension the Mormon Church. Residents expressed their frustration that they were having trouble voicing their concerns because the industrial livestock operation was connected with the inviolate sanctity of the church.

Problems of suppression also extend to scientific research. Since science is supposed to provide the foundation to public policy, agency action, and legal adjudication, it is critically important researchers be allowed the unfettered freedom to conduct their research and freely present their results. Indeed, this is the foundation of the tenure system for faculty in U.S. institutions of higher learning. Unfortunately, Adam Smith's invisible hand ostensibly guiding a free market economy appears too often supplanted by the iron fist of industry interests.

The anthropologist Walter Goldschmidt examined the effects of industrialized agriculture in the Central Valley of California beginning in the early 1940s. His work was sponsored by the Bureau of Agricultural Economics in the U.S. Department of Agriculture. Professor Goldschmidt painstakingly compared two similar towns, which differed in the extent to which they were surrounded by smaller independent farms versus larger corporate-owned operations. Goldschmidt found that the town surrounded by smaller independent farms had less poverty, more churches, more civic activity, better standard of living, more schools, more public recreation facilities, and more democratic governance. Thirty years later, in 1972, he provided Congressional testimony to a Senate Subcommittee "On The Role of Giant Corporations in the American and World Economies":

> I was ordered [in early 1940s] by my bureau chief in Washington not to undertake the second phase of the study. He did so in response to a buildup of pressure from politically powerful circles. These same sources of influence would have, as a matter of fact, prevented the publication of the report itself, had it not been for...the actions of the late Senator Murray of Montana. I was told, Mr. Senator and gentlemen, that the official manuscript of the study was literally in the file drawer of the desk occupied by Clinton Anderson, then the Secretary of Agriculture, and that it was released to Sena-

> tor Murray only upon his agreement that there would be no mention anywhere in the published report of the Department of Agriculture. I could regale this committee beyond its endurance with stories about this public pressure—as, for instance, our small research team being vilified on the radio each noon, as we ate our lunch...by the newscaster sponsored by the Associated Farmers of California. (Goldschmidt, 1972)

The Bureau sponsoring Goldschmidt's work was dismantled.

Unfortunately, Goldschmidt's experiences over a half century ago are still very much alive today. In the spring of 2002, I invited Dr. James Zahn, of the USDA Swine Research Center located at Iowa State University, to join me on a panel for a conference sponsored by the WaterKeeper Alliance and numerous other organizations. Dr. Zahn is one of the premier U.S. researchers engaged in identifying and understanding airborne emissions from large-scale swine operations. I invited him to present the results of his research. Despite Dr. Zahn's willingness to participate, his superiors within the USDA refused to allow him to join us. At Dr. Zahn's invitation, I appealed directly to Dr. Zahn's superiors to allow him to present his research. However, he was denied permission under the paltry excuse that the event was not an "appropriate venue." In my view, this shameful behaviour on the part of the USDA was little more than thinly veiled censorship, denying access to a publicly-funded researcher whose published works are centrally relevant for current public policy debates concerning the consequences for CAFOs on our environmental health.

Many independent family farmers in the U.S. are also discovering the very real consequences of tyranny and suppression by a centralized agricultural system. Farmers throughout the U.S. are forced to pay "tribute" to a centralized commodity organization when they market their products. In the pork industry, hog producers are required under the Federal Pork Production and Consumer Education Act (1985) to pay 45 cents out of every $100 of pork per hog sold, known as the pork check-off. Among the ostensible purposes of the money is the promotion of pork to U.S. consumers. However, many family hog farmers in the U.S. disagree with the advertising and public ideology created by these moneys. For example, they disagree with the promotion of pork as the "other white meat" because it may discourage the sale of bacon and ham. Or family farmers end up paying for messages that promote the sale of brand name meats by large-scale integrators as opposed to promoting family-farm-produced meats. Indeed, hog producers are essentially taxed some $50-60 million in check-off funds which are used to created and promote messages that may serve the interests of one segment of the industry over the other.

A legal challenge to this system was brought by the U.S. Campaign for Family Farms (CFF), which is an advocacy organization consisting of four sub-groups, including a substantial number of family hog farmers. CFF sought an end to the check-off program on the grounds that it was unconstitutional under the First Amendment because it essentially forced family hog producers to pay for messages they did not believe in or agree with. In other words, they are being compelled by the federal government to pay for messages to the general public concerning U.S. agriculture that they do not believe in. The case involved the CFF on one side against an opposition of *both* the Michigan Pork Producers (a state commodity organization funded, in part, by pork check-off funds) *and* the U.S. Department of Agriculture. In other words, a branch of the Federal Government, the U.S.D.A., purposefully blurred the distinction between private industry and public governance by allying itself with the Pork Check program to force farmers to pay financial tribute to the state in order that messages counter to family farm interests could be promoted to the general public. In October 2002, a U.S. District Court Judge thankfully ruled as follows:

> In days of low return on agricultural (sic), the decision of an individual farmer to devote funds to uses other than generic advertising is very important. Indeed, the frustration of some farmers are likely to only mount when those funds are used to pay for competitors' advertising, thereby depriving the farmer of the ability to pay for either niche advertising or

> non-advertising essentials (such as feed for 29 livestock). This is true regardless of whether objecting farmers are correct in their economic analysis that the assessments and speech do not sufficiently further their own particular interests. In short, whether this speech is considered on either philosophical, political or commercial grounds, it involves a kind of outrage which Jefferson loathed. The government has been made tyrannical by forcing men and women to pay for messages they detest. Such a system is at the bottom unconstitutional and rotten. For these reasons, the Court concludes that the mandated system of Pork Act assessments is unconstitutional since it violates the Cross-Plaintiffs' rights of free speech and association. (Enslen, 2002)

Discussion

Local maladies brought by industrial forms of agriculture leave community members and neighbourhoods frustrated, distraught, and dismayed. More disturbing than the odour, water quality degradation, neighbourhood social decay, or even the loss of family farms, is the realization by many that a government that should protect the public interests is frequently little more than a handmaiden of industrial agricultural interests. The larger cultural evolutionary and global contexts to these local and regional frustrations need to be brought to light so that the general public understands that its involvement in maintaining an equitable and sustainable food system is fundamental for ensuring a democratic society. Fixing the problem in any one neighbourhood's backyard should not mean chasing large-scale agricultural interests away to another neighbourhood, another region, another province, or another part of the world. Rather, addressing the litany of problems brought about by facilities such as Intensive Livestock Operations means courageous pioneering and homesteading on the political prairies. Otherwise, the following seemingly innocuous vision of a highly industrialized and centralized agriculture will have waves of consequences for the human order:

> To put an end to our backwardness in agriculture and to provide the country with the largest possible amount of market grain, cotton, and so forth, it was necessary to pass...to large-scale farming, for only large-scale farming can employ modern machinery, utilize all the achievements of agricultural science and provide the largest possible quantity of market produce...[We] took the path of organizing large farms...[This] method proved to be an exceedingly progressive method...particularly because it enabled us in the course of several years to cover the entire country with large farms capable of employing modern machinery, of utilizing all the achievements of agricultural science and of providing the country with the largest possible quantity of market produce. (Stalin, 1950)

The above excerpt comes from a speech delivered by Joseph Stalin in 1946 in Moscow at a meeting of voters of the Stalin Electoral District. It sounds eerily like the proponents of industrial agriculture in North America who, in ironic contrast to Stalin, promote large-scale agriculture via the rhetoric of "free markets" and "free trade." Whether cast as free market forces in North America, or as part of progressive development in the former Soviet Union, the rhetoric belies the political tyranny and wasteland created by industrial scale agriculture.

References

Barlett, P. (1989). Industrial agriculture. In S. Plattner (Ed.), *Economic anthropology* (pp. 253-291). Stanford: Stanford University Press.

Durrenberger, P., & Thu, K. (1998). Signals, systems, and environment in industrial food systems. *Journal of Political Ecology, 4*, 27-40.

Durrenberger, P., & Thu, K. (1996). The expansion of large scale hog farming in Iowa: The applicability of Goldschmidt's findings fifty years later. *Human Organization 55*(4), 409-415.

Enslen, R. (2002). *Michigan pork producers et al. v. campaign for family farms et al. v. Ann Venneman, Secretary of the U.S. Department of Agriculture.* Case #1:01-CV-34, U.S. District Court Western District of Michigan Southern Division. October 25. Kalamazoo, Michigan.

Flora, J., Hodne, C., Goudy, W., Osterberg, D., Kliebenstein, J., Thu, K., & Marquez, S. (2002). Social and community impacts. *Concentrated animal feeding operations air quality study,* pp. 147-163. Iowa State University and The University of Iowa Study Group Iowa City, Iowa: The University of Iowa.

Goldschmidt, W. (1947). *As you sow: How industrialize farming is changing the American way of life.* New York: Harcourt, Brace and Company.

Goldschmidt, W. (1972). *Testimony before the Senate Subcommittee on Big Business.* Washington, D.C.

Iowa State University and The University of Iowa Study Group (2002). *Concentrated animal feeding operations air quality study.* Iowa City: The University of Iowa.

Merchant, J., Kline, J., Donham, K., Bundy, D., & Hodne, C. (2002). Human health effects. *Concentrated animal feeding operations air quality study*, pp. 121-145. Iowa State University and The University of Iowa Study Group Iowa City, Iowa: The University of Iowa.

Minnesota State Legislature (2003). *Proposed amendment to Organic Transition Cost Share Bill.* State Capitol Minneapolis, Minnesota.

South Dakota Code (n.d.). *Disparagement.* Title 20, Chapter 20-10A.

Stalin, Joseph (1950). *Speech delivered by J. V. Stalin at a meeting of voters of the Stalin Electoral District, Moscow.* Moscow: Foreign Languages Publishing House.

Statistics Canada (n.d.). *Census of agriculture.*

Thu, K. (2002). Public health concerns for neighbours of large-scale swine production operations. *Journal of Agricultural Safety and Health 8*(2), 175-184.

Thu, K., & Durrenberger, P. (1994). North Carolina's hog industry: The rest of the story. *Culture and Agriculture 49*, 20-23.

Thu, K., & Durrenberger, P (Eds.). (1997). *Pigs, profits, and rural communities.* Albany, NY: State University of New York Press.

Thu, K., DeLind, L., Durrenberger, P., Flora, C., Flora, J., Heffernan, W., & Padgitt, S. (1996). Social issues. In K. Thu (Ed.), *Understanding the impacts of large-scale swine production: Proceedings from an Interdisciplinary Scientific Workshop*, pp.71-116. Iowa City: The University of Iowa.

Thu, K., Donham, K., Ziegenhorn, R., Reynolds, S., Thorne, P., Subramanian, P., Whitten, P., & Stookesberry, J. (1996). A control study of the physical and mental health of residents living near a large-scale swine operation. *Journal of Agricultural Safety and Health 3*(1), 13-26.

United States Department of Agriculture (n.d.). *National Agricultural Statistics Service*. [On-line]. Available: www.usda.gov/nass/pubs/histdata.htm.

Chapter 2
Corporate Livestock Production: Implications for Rural North America
by John Ikerd

North American agriculture is in the midst of a "great transition"—a transition that is fundamentally transforming rural areas. Agriculture as we have known it, with family farms and viable rural communities, is being rapidly transformed into an industrial agriculture, with factory farms and dying rural communities.

This industrialization of agriculture is not a new phenomenon. The trend toward specialization, standardization, and consolidation—toward industrialization—began around the turn of the 20th century, with the mechanization of agriculture. Until recently, the most obvious consequence of this process had been larger farms, fewer farms, and fewer farm families. But, farmers and families, real people, were still making the decisions concerning what was produced, how it was produced, and for whom it was produced. Today, however, these important decisions increasingly are made in the boardrooms of giant transnational corporations. These corporations are not real people; they have no families, no friends, no communities, and increasingly no single nationality. Their decisions are driven by the never-ending need to generate profits and to grow. The needs of families, communities, the land, and society in general, must be considered secondary to the needs of the corporation.

Nowhere is the industrialization more evident, in all of its dimensions and all of its ugliness, than in large-scale, confinement animal feeding operations (CAFOs) and in the corporations that control and promote them. One of the most repulsive aspects of corporate livestock production is the process by which contract production is promoted to the farmers and residents of rural North America. Farmers are told that these corporate contract operations will give young people an opportunity to return to the farm and told that significant government regulation of these CAFOs will deny rural youth their only opportunity. We should be critical of this assertion for several reasons.

First, the number of independent U.S. hog farmers has declined dramatically since the large-scale operations have become prominent, and most dramatically in those areas where CAFOs have been most prominent. The state of Missouri, for example, has lost about three-fourths of its hog farmers over the past decade, since large-scale contract operations first entered the state. The state of North Carolina preceded Missouri by doubling hog production, through CAFO operations, while cutting the number of independent hog producers in half. And the CAFO operations have been virtually unregulated. So unregulated corporate hog farms destroy opportunities for family hog farmers rather than create them—the facts on this are clear.

Second, contract hog production is not "farming;" it is a factory job that just happens to involve animals that have traditionally been raised on farms. Real farmers make their own decisions. Until recently, although farmers were becoming fewer and larger, farmers were still making all of the important production decisions, and most of these farmers considered how their decisions might affect the land and their neighbours. In contract livestock production, the corporation makes the decisions concerning design of buildings and equipment, genetics, feeding, animal health, time of placement, time of marketing, and virtually every other aspect of the production process. The corporation gives little consideration, if any, to the implications of these decisions for the land, the community, or even for the families of contract producers. A future in contract production is not a future in farming, no matter what corporate representatives or their lackeys in government or the state universities may say. Real farmers make their own decisions and accept the responsibilities for the impacts of their decisions on the land and on other people.

Third, it is difficult to understand why any parents would want their children to work in an unhealthy environment, to hire others to work in an unhealthy environment, or to impose an unhealthy environment on their neighbours. So, if parents want their children to become contract producers, it is difficult to understand why they would be opposed to regulations necessary to ensure their children's health and to protect the quality of the water and the air in rural areas. The only logical conclusion is that these parents want their children to live nearby and are willing to sacrifice the health of others to realize their own ambitions for their children.

Finally, there are other, better ways to farm and to raise hogs; the "sustainable agriculture" movement addresses the need to protect the rural environment and support rural communities, while providing opportunities for farmers to earn a decent living. But sustainable farming takes more imagination and creativity than contract production—it requires taking care of each other and taking care of the land. Sustainable hog producers all across North America are finding that deep-bedding systems, including hoop house structures and pasture based hog production systems, often are not only more humane, ecologically sound, and socially responsible, but also are more profitable than CAFOs. But such systems require more management, more imagination, more creativity, more thinking, and thus are more difficult to "promote" or to "control" from a distant, central location.

In a few years, the agribusiness corporations will leave North America, leaving their contract growers with useless investments in facilities, without "jobs," without farming skills, and with "big messes" for which they must be held responsible. The community will be left with nothing on which to base future economic development. But rural people do not seem to be willing to look that far ahead. They are lured by the corporate promises of more jobs, increased tax base, and the false promise of corporate livestock production as a viable future for farmers.

Every community is a bit different, but the fundamental issues are always the same. Some people in these communities expect to benefit economically by adopting an industrial model of livestock production, while others expect to suffer the inherently negative consequences of agricultural industrialization. Perhaps no public issue has so split the social fabric of rural communities, as when those who benefit economically confront those whose quality of life is diminished and the rest of the community is asked to choose sides.

The basic arguments are quite straightforward. Large-scale commercial hog producers, most operating under corporate contracts, feel compelled to adopt a factory model of production involving concentrated confinement housing, cesspool-like lagoon storage of hog feces and urine, and the spreading or spraying of manure on open fields. These producers claim that such operations represent a natural evolution of hog production and essentially are the same as any other family farming operation. Factory farming supporters argue that irrational and fanatical opponents are trying to deny their inherent "right to farm" and their right to pursue their economic interests in a free enterprise economy. They argue that, without compelling scientific proof of extraordinary risks to the environment or to human health, there is no reason to treat these factory livestock operations any differently than any other family farm.

However, common sense leads to a quite different conclusion. For example, all hog waste "lagoons" (cesspools) leak wastes into the groundwater. The only questions relate to how much they leak and how great a risk they present to human health. Inevitably, hog manure from these operations pollutes streams. The only questions relate to how many spills will occur in how many months and how great a risk they present to human health. All large confinement hog feeding operations stink. The only questions relate to how much of what chemicals are contained in the stench and how great a risk they present to human health. All large hog CAFOs rely on human antibiotics to control disease. The only questions relate to how much this contributes to antibiotic resistance in treating human diseases and how great a risk it presents to human health.

The common-sense answer to all of these questions is that the greater the number of hogs concentrated in one place, the greater will be the risk to the natural environment and, ultimately, the greater the risk to human health. Large-scale confinement animal feeding operations are not "farms" they are livestock factories. When hogs are raised on real farms, they are given sufficient space to move about, they spread their own waste—and, with common-sense management, do not pollute the groundwater or streams. When hogs are raised on real farms, they "smell," but do not "stink"—the difference being, "smell" does not make people sick. When hogs are raised on real farms, they need antibiotics only when they are sick, and generally, they stay healthy. The greater the number of hogs crowded into one building, on one farm, in one county, the greater will be the risk to human health. It is a matter of common sense.

Certainly commercial hog producers have a right to pursue their economic self-interest in a free enterprise economy. But they do not have a right to endanger the public health. "Private property rights" have never included the right to benefit at your neighbour's expense. The "right to farm" has never included the right to operate an "animal feeding factory."

The state and federal government agencies may feel compelled to wait for scientific proof, perhaps for a significantly large number of people to become disabled or die from hog-related illnesses. But at the local level, people have the responsibility of ensuring that they and their neighbours do not become those public health statistics. It is a contentious issue. People have no choice but to choose sides in this matter. Common sense—not economics and not science—should be our guide in deciding which side we should choose.

Recolonization of Rural North America

Today, rural North America is being "colonized." Transnational corporations are extending their economic sovereignty over the affairs of people in rural places everywhere. Corporate livestock production is but a symptom of a far more serious problem. Rural people are losing control of their local public institutions as outside corporate interests, previously alien to their communities, use their economic power to gain controlling influence over local economies and local governments. Irreplaceable precious rural resources, including rural people and rural culture, are being exploited to increase the wealth of investors and managers of corporations that have no commitment to the future of their "rural colonies." This is classic "colonization."

Historically, a colony has been defined as a territory acquired by conquest or settlement, over which a people or government, previously alien to that territory, has imposed outside control. A colonial relationship existed whenever one people or government extended its sovereignty by imposing political control over another people or territory. The only fundamental difference between the current colonization of rural areas and previous colonization of "lesser developed" countries is the nature of the entity carrying out the process—the source of power. Historically, colonization has been carried out by political entities, by governments. Today, colonization is being carried out by economic entities, by transnational corporations. However, the colonization process and its consequences are virtually identical, regardless of the source of power.

Rural people, whether in North America or elsewhere, are being told that they must rely on outside investment, like corporate livestock producers, to support local economic development. They are also informed that outside investment will bring badly needed jobs and income, stimulate the local economy, and expand the local tax base. Economically depressed rural communities will be able to afford better schools, better health care, and expanded social services, and will attract a greater variety of retail outlets—restaurants, movie theatres, and maybe even a Wal-Mart. Their rural community will begin to look more like an urban community and local people will begin to think and act more like urban people. Rural people have been left behind, they are told, and outside corporate investment is the only means by which they can advance fast enough to catch up with the rest of society.

These same basic arguments have been used by the powerful of all times to justify their colonization of the weak. Colonization was the only feasible means of improving the lives of the "natives" left behind in "primitive" societies—economically, socially, and morally underdeveloped. Since the indigenous people had no adequate means of developing their resources themselves, it was only fair they give up some of the benefits to the colonizing nation in order to acquire the outside investment needed for the development process. It was a "win-win" situation, or so they were told.

Historically, the British, Spanish, Portuguese, French, Germans, and Dutch were among the great empire builders. They colonized much of North, South, and Central America, Australia, and Africa, as well as major regions of Asia. Through colonization, the "primitive" people already occupying these territories were given an opportunity to become a part of a modern society. After failing to gain cooperation through persuasion, the leaders of the indigenous "tribes" were invariably bribed, threatened, or coerced into colluding with the colonizing powers. After all, it was for the ultimate good of "their people." The 19th century empire builders, in particular, claimed they had a moral responsibility to help bring "backward people" some of the fruits of modern Western civilization. And, if the "natives" continued to resist, they were subdued by force and their indigenous cultures destroyed—for their own good, of course.

Clearly, becoming part of a colonial empire brought numerous economic, health, education, and technological benefits to past colonies. In some cases, such as North America and Australia, the indigenous population was sufficiently small to be effectively dominated by immigrants who shared the culture of their colonial masters. Some colonies became strong enough to gain independence, and a few are now more powerful than are their one-time masters. But most colonies were not granted independence until well into the 20th century, when world opinion shifted against colonialism on ethical and moral grounds.

According to contemporary standards of international behaviour, colonialism is inexcusable because it conflicts directly with the basic rights of national sovereignty and self-determination. The recognition of such rights, worldwide, ended political colonialism as a means of promoting economic and cultural development. Political colonialism was abolished worldwide, because it had obvious harmful effects on the people of colonized areas—socially, culturally, ecologically, and economically. Long-established social lifestyles were suddenly disrupted, complete cultures were destroyed, natural resources were extracted, and the natural environment was degraded under colonization.

After the colonizers had completed their exploitation, the local economy was left in shambles with no indigenous community structure or any other means of self-government to address the shameful legacy of colonialism. In spite of the occasional economic benefits to the colonized, the indigenous people of virtually every previously colonized country of the world, including the United States and Canada, still harbour a deep resentment of their former colonial masters. Political colonization is no longer morally or ethically excusable.

However, the "corporate colonization" of rural areas everywhere, including North America, continues virtually unchecked. The earliest colonial intrusions into rural areas were motivated by exploitation of its abundant wildlife, vast forest lands, and precious mineral deposits—invariably leaving behind frontier "ghost towns" after the wealth had been extracted from the land. More recently, intrusions have been motivated by the exploitation of cheap rural labour by the textile and food processing industries, for example. But, once the corporations found people who would work even harder for less money in other countries, the textile industry moved on, leaving behind deserted factories and unemployable people. With the creation of the North American Free Trade Agreement (NAFTA), the food processing industry now seems likely to abandon North America to colonize rural Mexico instead. However, corporate colonialism continues in rural areas to exploit remaining pockets of valuable rural resources, including an agricultural work ethic, trusting communities, and open spaces in which to dump various kinds of noxious wastes that urban people have rejected.

Today, corporate livestock production provides a prime example of corporate colonization of rural North America. Local people are promised new jobs, more income, an expanded tax base, and an opportunity to "catch up" with the rest of North American society. Local leaders are courted or coerced, as necessary, to shape local policies to accommodate industrial hog production methods. Local farmers are told industrialization is the wave of the future for agriculture and they must embrace the new technologies to survive. Rural people are told that local regulations to protect the public health and natural environment will drive existing farmers out of business, will stifle economic development, and will doom their community to continued "backwardness." These arguments are no different from past arguments used to support political colonization; only the source of power is different.

In reality, few local people will gain from such colonization. A few local officials and land speculators may line their pockets and a few local people may get relatively good paying jobs, for a time. But, nearly all of the profits and good paying jobs will go to corporate investors and managers who will remain outside the community. Most rural North Americans eventually will refuse to work for exploitative employers, leaving most of the low-paying jobs to be filled by immigrant labour. Eventually, the colonizing corporations will move on, once local resources have been depleted or local resistance to their exploitation begins to affect their bottom line. Perhaps some post-colonial rural communities will be prosperous, but these so-called success stories will be limited to places with unique landscapes and climates deemed worthy of preserving for the enjoyment of affluent outsiders.

As in earlier times, the 21st century corporate empire builders claim they feel some responsibility to help bring "backward people" of rural areas some of the benefits of the modern economy. However, rural people are not necessarily "backward" just because they have not embraced the exploitative system of industrial development and have been reluctant to discard their traditional rural cultural values. After the corporations are gone, there is no reason to believe that rural North Americans will be less resentful of their previous "corporate colonial masters" than are indigenous people of previously colonized nations of their previous "political colonial masters." They will resent the loss of rural culture, rural values, and their previous sense of connectedness to place. They will resent the loss of a once safe and healthy rural environment in which they had hoped to live and raise their families. They will resent the loss of their self-governing ability, as their communities will have been split apart by dissension during the colonizing process. They will resent the loss of their sense of community.

The threat of colonization is always present. The economically and politically powerful will always be tempted to dominate and exploit the weak. However, differences in economic and political power only make colonization possible—not necessary or inevitable. The powerful can be restrained from their natural tendency to expand their sovereignty over the weak, and even if they are not, the weak can always find ways to resist the powerful.

The strongest defense rural North America has against the threat of corporate colonization is the knowledge of what is happening to their communities, why it is happening, and what the consequences will be of their doing nothing to stop it. The colonization of rural areas is not inevitable. But rural residents must stand together to preserve their priceless rural culture, to protect their valuable natural and human resources, and pursue a different strategy of "sustainable" rural economic development. First, however, the people of rural North America must come to realize that corporate livestock production is not a solution to their problems, but instead is an exploitative response to their growing desperation. The solution for rural North Americans is not to submit to corporate colonization, but instead to declare their economic independence and begin rebuilding their own communities from the grass-roots.

Chapter 3
Pork, Politics, and Power
by Fred Tait

Pork, politics, and power—this mixture of ingredients, when applied in rural communities, can generate a toxic mix that damages the environment, erodes democracy, compromises people's organisations, discredits our civil service, and divides and disrupts communities.

The story of pork, politics, and power is the story of the corporate takeover of Canadian hog production and the effects of unrestrained economic power on governments and communities. The transnational-controlled hog mega-barns of today are just one example of the growing corporate control of agriculture in Canada—where transnational giants are taking control of every aspect of the food system that can be adapted to their model. To understand the situation today, we must first look at the past to understand how much hog production and marketing have been altered.

Single-desk Selling and its Origins

In the 1960s and the 1970s, Manitoba hog farmers were struggling within a market-system that worked against them. Farmers who wanted to sell hogs could not find out the price that packers and other buyers were paying for similar animals (there was no "price transparency"). Individual farmers received different prices for products of equal value. And there were deals made between middlemen and packers. Hog farmers demanded fairer market conditions. As a result, the National Farmers Union (NFU) led the battle to establish a system called "single-desk selling."

Farmers won their battle in 1972 when Manitoba's first NDP government, under Premier Ed Schreyer, created the Manitoba Hog Producers Marketing Board with its single-desk selling powers. To implement single-desk selling, farmers and government worked together to put in place a producer-controlled marketing structure: any packer who wanted to purchase hogs had to buy from that single-desk seller. Single-desk selling gave farmers total price transparency, equal access to the market, an equal price for products of equal value, and market power when dealing with packers.

During the decades that single-desk selling was in place, and until recently, hog production was well dispersed across the province and production was largely in the hands of small and medium-sized farmers. There was very little conflict between hog farmers and local residents. And hog production followed market signals: when grain prices went up, hog prices went down; farmers adjusted production; and we had—though clearly not perfect—some equilibrium in the production system.

The End of Single-desk Selling

In 1996, Harry Enns—then Manitoba's Minister of Agriculture in the Filmon Conservative Government—arbitrarily ended single-desk selling of hogs with a stroke of a pen. Governments in Saskatchewan, Alberta, and Ontario did likewise—unilaterally terminated farmers' single-desk selling agencies. In Manitoba, Enns proceeded against enormous opposition from hog farmers. Farmers loudly voiced their opposition at meetings, and a survey by Manitoba Pork in 1995 indicated that 76% of farmers in Manitoba opposed the end of the single-desk.

Enns justified his move against farmers saying that he wanted to attract a "world-class" hog packing plant to the province, and that he wanted to create competition within the hog industry. "Competition," it turns out, means that farmers must compete with one another to supply lower cost hog "inputs" to packing plants. As Enns wished, Manitoba now has a world-class packing plant, Maple Leaf's. That plant now kills and processes most of the hogs processed in Manitoba. The irony is that Enns' actions transformed Manitoba from having a single-desk *seller* to having virtually a single-desk *buyer*. The results for farmers are predictable: they receive less while producing more, and in many cases they are forced out of production altogether.

Maple Leaf Foods Inc. in Brandon

In February 1998, Maple Leaf Foods Inc. announced that it would build a world-class $112 million hog-packing plant in the city of Brandon. Maple Leaf is owned by one branch of the McCain family. Maple Leaf's 2002 revenues were over $5 billion. It is Canada's largest pork processor. Landmark Feeds, a Maple Leaf subsidiary, is Western Canada's largest animal nutrition company. Maple Leaf's Elite Swine produces over 2.75 million hogs per year.

Maple Leaf's Brandon plant would have a capacity to slaughter 4.5 million hogs annually (operating at maximum capacity). The Conservative government of the day refused to hold the customary Clean Environment Commission hearings despite the scale of the project, despite the attendant need to increase Manitoba hog production by perhaps two million hogs per year (probably raised in mega-barns), despite questions about the discharge of wastewater containing nitrogen and phosphorous from the manure removed from the slaughtered hogs, and despite numerous requests from citizens. Without hearings, the province granted a licence to build the kill and processing plant and also for the wastewater treatment plant that would discharge into the Assiniboine River.

The city of Brandon, a major player in this whole enterprise, signed an agreement with Maple Leaf that the city would build the wastewater treatment plant at taxpayers' expense: an estimated $6-to-$7 million. The city also agreed to pay Maple Leaf for any losses that resulted from packing plant shutdowns caused by any failure of the wastewater treatment system—a costly risk for the city.

Luckily, provincial officials effectively ensured that the city of Brandon would never be put in the expensive situation of having to compensate Maple Leaf for shutdown costs. Provincial officials did so by assigning to the city the responsibility for monitoring the quality of water in the Assiniboine River downstream from the Maple

Leaf plant. Cearly, the city of Brandon cannot afford to find problems with the water quality in the Assiniboine River.

There were other pitfalls. In its wisdom, the province decided that it was not necessary to construct a treatment plant that could remove phosphorous from the slaughter-plant wastewater. Today, tests of the effluent from the Maple Leaf plant show phosphorus content up to seven times the predicted levels, and tests indicate highly elevated phosphorous levels in the Assiniboine River downstream of the Maple Leaf plant (Patton, n.d.).

When Brandon finished building a wastewater treatment plant for Maple Leaf, the city faced a significant cost over-run. The final cost almost doubled the initial estimate of $6-to-$7 million. Far worse, however, Maple Leaf looked at the finished product and, in effect, said: "Well that's very nice, but there's a problem, you must have misunderstood: You've build a wastewater treatment plant to serve one shift and we intend to go to two." Thus, Brandon's final cost over-run (Maple Leaf has announced that it will add a second shift in 2004) may be in excess of $20 million. This will be a heavy burden for a city of 30,000 people.

The subsidies to the Maple Leaf's Brandon plant continue to mount but so far include:

- Hog farmers are subsidizing the plant through lower hog prices resulting from the termination of single-desk selling.
- The environment is subsidizing the plant as rivers and lakes struggle to absorb the phosphorous from the plant and the phosphorous and nitrogen from the hog mega-barns that supply the plant.
- The people of Brandon are subsidizing Maple Leaf by paying for the waste-water treatment plant and, soon, its expansion, as well as through business tax breaks and by providing the land for the plant for $1 (Chambers, n.d.).
- The province of Manitoba is subsidizing the plant by contributing about $11 million for sewers, roads, and a worker training plan.
- The federal government contributed $3 million in subsidies.
- Workers across Canada are subsidizing the plant through lower wages—brought down by a joint program of Maple Leaf and

> the province of Manitoba to bring in migrant Mexican workers. This is necessary because insufficient numbers of Canadians would work in the plant due to low wages and poor working conditions. In addition, beginning in 1995, Maple Leaf and other corporate packers began a string of lock-outs and labour disputes and forced their workers to take wage rollbacks of up to 40%. These rollbacks will reduce Maple Leaf's labour costs at its Brandon plant enough to pay for the \$112 million cost of that plant every six years.

In addition, there are the costs, borne by taxpayers, of dealing with a poorly-paid, transient workforce—policing, social services, addictions counselling, health care, workers' compensation, and family abuse.

The Struggle to Re-establish Single-desk Selling

So Brandon got its hog plant and farmers lost single-desk selling. But farmers' struggle to restore their single-desk went on.

The Conservative government that had removed single-desk selling for hogs was defeated in the general election of September 1999 and replaced with the present New Democratic Party (NDP) government of Premier Gary Doer. Because the NDP, when in opposition, had opposed the end of single-desk selling and promised to reinstate it if New Democrats got elected (Bell, 2000), farmers were optimistic that an injustice would soon be reversed.

Soon after the NDP's 1999 election win, NFU member Ken Sigurdson and I drove to Winnipeg to meet with Rob Hilliard, the President of the Manitoba Federation of Labour. We told Mr. Hilliard that a great injustice had been done to farmers. Farmers' collective marketing power was arbitrarily taken away from them. We said to him,

> This injustice must be repaired, because single-desk selling for farmers is equivalent to collective-bargaining rights for labour. We want organized labour's support to restore sin-

> gle-desk selling in this province. Now that we have a government back in power that will be supportive of the principle of farmers and workers having collective bargaining power, we need to push this issue, and the best place to push it is at the upcoming NDP Convention.

We got a very good hearing from Rob Hilliard.

In February of 2000, in Brandon, the Manitoba NDP held its first Convention after forming government. As luck would have it, the NDP invited me to speak on an agricultural panel at their convention. I was there as a guest. On the first evening, Ken Sigurdson moved an emergency resolution to support the restoration of single-desk selling for hogs. The Convention chair declared that the resolution carried by the required two-thirds majority and right away there was a challenge to the chair. A standing vote was called.

I was sitting at a table—in the right place, it turned out—and just by accident, I overheard a convention delegate urging his people: "Make sure everybody is in this room. We have to defeat this resolution." At the time, I did not know the gentleman who was giving those instructions. The standing vote was called, and the motion to allow the emergency resolution was defeated. The person I had heard giving instructions to his delegates to defeat the motion turned out to be none other than Bernie Christophe, then President of the United Food and Commercial Workers (UFCW) Union in Manitoba. The UFCW is the union that represents almost all of Manitoba's packing plant workers. Christophe spoke against the resolution. To add insult to injury, Rob Hilliard failed to have the Manitoba Federation of Labour (MFL) delegates vote in favour of the resolution. Most voted against it. And so, in that vote, an alliance in this country that had lasted for perhaps 60 years—that had lasted from at least the beginning of the CCF, and probably from before that; an alliance of workers and farmers struggling together in a common front to create a better society—suddenly was divided. That alliance of farmers and labour was betrayed.

We did not give up after the defeat of our resolution at the 2000 NDP convention. The next year, we took another run at it; because we were determined that justice for farmers should prevail. In preparation for the 2001 convention, Ken, myself, and other NFU members again worked very diligently, doing a lot of background work—meeting and lobbying. And we went to that second convention, this time in Winnipeg, and moved another emergency resolution.

Just prior to that convention, Manitoba Minister of Agriculture Rosann Wowchuk called a meeting of selected farm leaders, in Portage La Prairie. And there she said: "The Premier is starting to change his position. He's at a point where I think he will probably accept single-desk selling as long as we don't push him too hard on the issue."

Seeing that the minister was doing her best to restore single-desk selling, I thought she could use all the support she could get. So Ken Sigurdson and I moved our second emergency resolution and got strong support. Again, we needed a two-thirds majority to get the resolution accepted and to refer it to a vote. This time, we got almost unanimous support: the party structure had been caught off guard by the mistaken belief that we had been placated by Minister Wowchuk's assurances that the premier was starting to change his position on single-desk selling. Our resolution would go to the convention floor.

When the resolution was debated the following day, the Minister of Agriculture spoke against it and moved an amendment that would require the province's hog producers to call for a vote to restore single-desk selling. The amended resolution passed, with the government and others knowing well that a hog farmer could not publicly involve him- or herself in any campaign to restore single-desk selling without putting at risk his or her hog production contract with Maple Leaf as well as access to the market.

After the debate on the resolution was over, a *Winnipeg Free Press* reporter named Helen Fallding asked Manitoba Premier Gary Doer about his reaction to the vote and the divisive issue. Premier Doer responded by saying that he had promised Maple Leaf Foods President Michael McCain that there would be no return to single-desk marketing in Manitoba (Fallding, 2001).

When we think about that promise to Michael McCain, we have to consider that Michael McCain is not a resident of Manitoba. He's neither a member of, nor a major contributor to, the New Democratic Party: in fact, he represents everything that the founders of the movement would have opposed. Yet a promise was made to Michael McCain that overwhelms all of the province's history and the dedication of the people who fought for progressive policies in this province. While meeting with Premier Doer behind closed doors, McCain was able to compromise a legacy reaching as far back as the general strike of 1919. That legacy includes the heritage of J. S. Woodsworth, Stanley Knowles, and M. J. Coldwell; the creation of the CCF; the proud legacy of Manitoba farm leaders Jake Shultz and Max Hoffer; and former Premiers Ed Schreyer and Howard Pawley. In this one meeting, the long struggle of farmers to gain market power and single-desk selling was reversed. This historic transfer of power had taken place without prior public debate or a mandate from the electorate. We must now realistically consider the possibility that this new alliance of government, business, and labour will at some time in the future be tempted to silently agree to the termination of farmers' supply management agencies or the Canadian Wheat Board.

Michael McCain was able to compromise all that history, all those community meetings in the 1960s and 70s, all that effort to bring about single-desk selling and to gain marketing power for farmers. The man whose company stood to make millions in profits from lower hog prices ultimately decided whether farmers would enjoy the market power of single-desk selling.

Key Union Leaders Oppose Single-desk Selling

It is clear why Michael McCain might work against farmers, why he might oppose farmers' right to bargain collectively. It is less clear, however, why some labour unions would do so (some unions, such as the Grain Services Union, have stood in solidarity with farmers). One has to wonder then, what has happened here? Why would representatives of organized labour break their long-standing alliance with farmers? Part of the answer may be the Crocus Investment Fund: a labour-sponsored investment capital fund in Manitoba. Rob Hilliard, president of the Manitoba Federation of Labour, is also the chair of the board of directors of the Crocus Fund. And the Crocus Fund is a major investor ($1.8 million) in a company called Enterprise Swine Ltd. and a major investor ($900,000) in Turtle Mountain Pork. (Both the Enterprise and Turtle Mountain operations are operated by Dynamic Pork, a joint venture of N. M. Patterson & Sons and Manitoba Pork.)

Mega-barn investments by a labour-sponsored investment fund chaired by the President of the Manitoba Federation of Labour raises a number of questions. Currently, workers in hog mega-barns are exempted from Manitoba's *Employment Standards Act*. Have the Crocus Fund and the Manitoba Federation of Labour used their investment to raise working standards for its hog barn workers? Did the Crocus Fund directors use their investment to change the industry-standard practice of applying manure based on a crop's nitrogen needs (and, in so doing, over-applying phosphorus)? Did the Crocus Fund directors make their investment so that they could demonstrate a superior model of manure storage: an alternative to digging a hole in the dirt, filling it full of hog manure, and calling it leading-edge technology and best-of-industry practice? These are rather embarrassing questions, I suspect. In correspondence, the Crocus Fund finally replied that, in its investments, it adopted leading-edge technology. But what is leading-edge technology in the mega-barn sector? It is that you underpay your labour, and employ them under the farm labour code. You put your manure in a hole in the ground because that is the cheapest system. There is virtually no difference between the way that Crocus-funded barns are raising hogs and the way that other corporate mega-barns are raising hogs.

The labour movement put itself in a terrible conflict of interest by investing in corporate hog production. The Crocus Fund's return on that investment would be affected by the costs of running its operations. So, with its investments, Crocus acquired an interest in seeing that the costs of running its barns were not increased as a result of stringent environmental regulations or proper labour codes.

The other factor that may have undermined the judgment of many in the labour movement and caused them to work against farmers' interests was the prospect of Maple Leaf's Brandon plant employing 1,100 people on a single shift. These workers would be union members. Better yet, these workers would be largely a transient labour force that would move through the system (the worker turnover rate at the Brandon plant in the first year was well in excess of 100% and it has continued to escalate). And for some union leaders, that is a desirable situation: If you have got a stable, long-term labour force, they become unruly and start talking about changes to contracts and to union leadership. With the Brandon plant, the union in charge, the UFCW, would get the dues from 1,100 workers continually changing through the plant, and from an additional 900 workers when a second shift is added. Almost the entire labour movement in Manitoba has been silent on this issue and seems willing to accept indentured labour.

Mega-barns and Standards in Manitoba

Clearly, Michael McCain, the Manitoba government, and many in the Manitoba labour movement wanted the Brandon packing plant and its 1,100 to 2,000 jobs. But what about the barns needed to supply that plant? What will be the impact of the millions of pigs and the hundreds of corporate mega-barns on rural Manitoba and on the Manitoba environment?

The Crocus Fund and the Manitoba Federation of Labour tried to justify their investments by talking about "leading-edge" technology and better standards, when all along they were just following the mega-barn model that has proved so damaging in the U.S. and elsewhere. The Manitoba government similarly tries to pretend that standards in Manitoba are significantly higher than standards in North Carolina and other jurisdictions where the proliferation of hog mega-barns has meant fouled rivers, contaminated wells, the expulsion of family farmers, and divided rural communities.

Staff in Manitoba's Departments of Intergovernmental Affairs, Agriculture, and Conservation have repeatedly assured me that, "We're not going to make the same mistakes here in Manitoba that were made in North Carolina." The Minister of Agriculture told me, "We're going to do things different here in Manitoba."

The refrain from every department and level of government is that Manitoba has the "the best regulations in Canada." Often, carried away by enthusiasm, they declare: "We've got the best regulations in North America."

And how does this "best-regulations-in-North-America" system work? A proponent designs a project, picks a location, draws up the diagrams of the earthen storage and of the actual barn construction, and so on. The proponent puts all this information into a proposal with all the engineering data and presents it to a local municipal council. Provincial officials assume that local municipal councillors do not have the expertise to assess such complex proposals, and so the municipalities are urged to pass the proposal to one of the province's Technical Review Teams. The Technical Review Teams are made up of civil servants from Agriculture, Intergovernmental Affairs, and Conservation. Team members look at the technical and design aspects of the proposed barns and then send the proposal back to the local council with a recommendation. There has never been a case, to my knowledge, where a Technical Review Team has rejected a proposal. The Teams always say that the proposal "meets or exceeds" guidelines. The Technical Review Team may say that it has "concerns" with one aspect or another, but it never rejects a proposal. Often, after these proposals come back from the Technical Review Team, dedicated individuals working with HogWatch Manitoba take these proposals apart, word by word. I will give you some examples of the errors that we find.

I was involved with groups opposing a proposal to build a barn north of Portage La Prairie. The Technical Review Team approved the project. Two of the civil servants on the Technical Review Team were sitting in the cafeteria in the provincial building in Portage La Prairie and were overheard saying: "I don't know why those people are opposing that project. We reviewed that proposal and it meets and exceeds every requirement that the province has. They're wasting their time. They haven't a hope of defeating this proposal."

Despite the endorsement of the project and its details by that Review Team, at the next stage—the conditional use hearing that the municipality must hold—we pointed out to the municipal council that the drawings of the earthen storage lagoon were technically wrong. We pointed out to the council that the capacity of the manure lagoon, listed in the report as large enough to hold 400 days of manure, was wrong: it could not hold 400 days' worth of manure. We showed the council that the soil permeability tests—a key determining factor in whether a lagoon will leak—were not calculated correctly. Some of us joked that this was probably why the lagoon was built undersized—because they knew it was going to leak! And we pointed out to the council that the text said that there would be a cold storage area in the barn to store mortalities: but the blueprints showed no such facility in the barn. And the Technical Review Team had missed it all. The system had failed. The council wrote a scathing report critical of the Technical Review Team work, and further recognized the work of citizen groups that had identified the flaws in the proponent's material that had helped the council come to the unanimous decision to reject the proposal.

And the Portage barn is not an isolated incident. There have been other instances where people, lay people, have taken apart these proposals for barns and found numerous flaws that were missed by the Technical Review Teams. So we asked the Technical Review people: "What's going on? How come you missed these errors?" We got a letter saying that Technical Review Team members "are not required to check the proponent's material for accuracy." Well, if the Technical Review Team does not check for accuracy, who does? It should not be up to a bunch of ordinary citizens, scattered around rural communities, to analyze and check all this technical data in order to protect the public good and the environment. It seems to me, as taxpayers, in a democracy, that we should employ independent public servants to do that work.

Increasingly, however, we do not employ independent public servants to do research, to test for safety, or to assess the accuracy of data submitted by corporations. When we look at Agriculture and Agri-Food Canada and the procedures they use to license veterinary drugs, we see that we have reduced funding and staffing at our independent public labs, and that the remaining scientists are reduced to reviewing data submitted by the proponent corporations. Increasingly, in all parts of our food safety and environmental protection system, the developer's or the proponent's material is given to people in the various branches of the public service to accept and these public servants are denied an opportunity to do their own research or tests to verify that data. Our public servants cannot protect the public interest. The government has reduced these public servants to legitimizing something that does not have legitimacy. This has put incredible pressure on these public servants. We have people out on stress leave and others threatening to resign. This mixture of pork, politics, and power is destroying these people's credibility in their community and putting this stress upon them. And it is destroying the safety and regulatory systems that we rely on as citizens, as well as helping to destroy the public's trust in government.

A barn built near Souris provides another example of how Manitoba's approval system breaks down. Because the soil where the barn was to be built was very porous, the engineer stated that the manure storage pit would need a clay liner. After construction, the engineer issued an engineering certificate that this earthen manure storage pit was built to the proper standard, that there was a clay liner put into the pit, and that it met all the provincial guidelines. And so the province then issued a license to operate the mega-barn and the manure storage pit. Local residents said, "That's darn strange. How could they put a clay liner in that pit without any trucks hauling clay in there?" Nobody from the civil service went and looked at the site or the pit; they just accepted the data from the proponent and the engineer. The barn had gone into operation in November and by April there was no liquid in the lagoon—it had all gone into the aquifer.

As a third example, we had a proposal in 2001 near Dauphin called CanMark Family Farms (the "Can" and the "Mark" in the name refer to Canada and the barn's investors from Denmark). Provincial regulations say that when you will build your manure storage pit that you must strip off all the top soil, you must put your earth liner into the pit in six inch layers, you must pack it to certain densities, and you must have no rocks over six inches in diameter. A local farmer, Charles Beer, was out at the construction site every day. It was just after harvest when the contractor started building the manure storage pit. The contractor did not even bother burning the swath and the stubble off. They never stripped the topsoil. And they buried rocks up to 30 inches in diameter. The local farmer filmed the lagoon construction every day, and he complained to the Department of Conservation. Department officials came out and said that the contractor would have to tear the lagoon up and rebuild it. The Conservation official went back to Brandon and the contractor put the lagoon back together exactly the same as it was the first time. Today, that lagoon is licensed and operating.

As a final example, on July 21, 2002 at 9:15 p.m., near the community of McGregor, Manitoba, not far from where I live, an above-ground, steel manure storage tank burst. A million gallons of hog slurry dropped out onto sandy soil. Soon, all that was left on the surface was the solids: the rest entered the aquifer. Two wells in the immediate area were contaminated.

We did not know any of this right away; Manitoba's Department of Conservation is not required to report manure spills to the public. About 10 days after the accident, a reporter told me that he had received an anonymous call that something went wrong at McGregor. He gave me a land location and I drove over. You could see what had happened. The media jumped all over the issue and the government and the industry attempted damage control. They said, "Yes, there was a spill, but the system worked, because the spill was reported within an hour and fifteen minutes." What they did not tell the public, however, was that prior to the spill they had not known that the barn or storage tank was there. The government in Manitoba claims that it has the best regulations in North America, but it doesn't even know where most of the barns are, because any barn built before 1998 in Manitoba was not licensed, and thus not recorded.

That manure storage in McGregor was a salvaged tank from some other operation in the U.S. It was brought into Manitoba and reassembled. Robert Kozuch, president of Engineered Storage Products, the firm that originally manufactured the tank, issued a news release on August 23, 2002 that said: "The failure of this structure is an unfortunate incident and it should not have occurred...We believe that the failure of this tank was due to gross negligence on the part of the contractor that assembled the tank." I would contend that the incident also exposes gross negligence on the part of the government that should have regulated the building of that tank and should have known where it was.

Mega-barns and the Family Farm

Hog mega-barns damage the environment, and they are equally damaging to family farms. In 1991, there were 2,969 hog producers in Manitoba. In 2001, just 1,379 remained: a loss of 54% in 10 years.

The 1,379 hog producers that remain produced, in 2001, 6,350,000 hogs. These hogs had a total market value of $860 million. Agriculture Ministers just love to get up and rattle off these kinds of statistics. But Ministers and other mega-barn promoters leave out some important information. Manitoba's *Farmers' Independent Weekly* reported that 11% of those producers, just 152 in total, produced 82% of all those hogs. Those 152 operations, that 11% of hog producers, produced 5,270,000 of those hogs. Those 152 operations earned $705 million, for an average earning per operation of $4.6 million. Now there is a family farm!

For the other 1,227 producers, their gross earnings from hog production averaged $126,000 each. It would require very few additional operations the size of the big 152 to occupy all the space in the market that those other 1,227 small producers currently supply.

The makeup of the hog production sector directly affects the makeup of the Manitoba Pork Council, the organization that, in theory, works on behalf of those 1,227 smaller hog producers. The Manitoba Pork Council collects an 85¢ per-head check-off on market hogs and a 20¢ per head check-off on export weanlings. This gives the Council a total budget of over $3 million per year. And just as those 152 large operations produce 82% of the hogs in Manitoba, these 152 large operations contribute 82% of the Manitoba Pork Council's budget. Those 152 producers, because of their contribution to the organization, have significant influence on the policy statements and the political work of the Council.

One of the things that the Manitoba Pork Council—and the marketing arm, the Manitoba Pork Marketing Co-op Inc.—does with that $3 million per year is to run a public relations campaign on behalf of its large producers. This campaign includes clever television ads. One ad shows a farm family out playing in its yard, kicking a soccer ball. The husband walks over to an open-air, hoop-style hog shelter. His hogs are happy, playing on straw bedding, and he wanders around among them and talks about what a great thing the hog industry is. What a beautiful picture: not a mega-barn or a manure lagoon in sight. What a deceptive picture: the 82% of Manitoba's hogs that come from those 152 large operations never come near an open-air barn or near straw bedding. And the big packers are going out of their way to ensure that hogs in the future will *never* come near to the open air or to straw: Maple Leaf Foods has indicated that in the near future, it will not purchase hogs from any open-air system because, it claims, of the fear that birds could introduce salmonella and stray cats could introduce toxoplasmosis into the hog herd. Thus, not only is the pork industry's television ad—open-air barns and happy hogs—not representative of most of Manitoba's hog production, but these "producer groups" are working with packers to ensure that the scene depicted in their ads will disappear completely from the Manitoba countryside. It is easy to predict the negative effects on smaller, family farm hog producers when Maple Leaf stops buying hogs from anyone with an open-air barn.

So the big packers and the big barns do not seem very beneficial to the farm families that produce, or formerly produced, hogs. The other argument that we hear, however, in rural Manitoba and rural Saskatchewan and rural Alberta, is that these mega-barns will create a new market for feed grain and thus increase the price for grain farmers. This argument is false because it ignores the economic fact that grain prices in rural Manitoba, rural Saskatchewan, and rural everyplace, will be world price backed off for freight. To understand this, ask: How will mega-barn owners determine what to pay for feed grain? Answer: they will match, perhaps with a nickel-or-two premium, what the farmer would get from the alternative market. The alternative market is the export market, the world market. But to access that world market, a farmer in Manitoba would have to pay the rail freight bill to Vancouver or Thunder Bay. In the alternative market, the world market, the farmer would get world price less freight costs. The mega-barns match this price. Thus, with or without hog mega-barns, the price of feed grain in Manitoba will be world price less freight.

Conclusions

So what do we have in Manitoba, this province with the "highest hog production standards in North America," perhaps in the world? We have a packing plant in Brandon that the government decided could release its wastewater into the river without removing the phosphorous. We have water quality in the river monitored by a financially-strapped city that is required to pay Maple Leaf if water quality problems force the packing plant to suspend operations. We have substandard hog lagoons and manure tanks that leak and spill manure slurry which then gets into the groundwater and surface water.

We have civil servants on stress leave because they are not allowed to properly examine data submitted by proponent corporations. We have regulators that do not even know the locations of the barns that they are supposed to monitor.

We have a government that refuses to reinstate farmers' single-desk selling advantage because of a promise made to the owner of the biggest packing plant. And we have open season on family farm hog producers.

We have labour leaders turned against farmers, breaking a generations-old alliance with farmers and actually investing in the mega-barns that are wiping out family farms, all in order to gain higher returns on investments.

And we have parasitic corporate industrial operations extracting the wealth from rural areas and, most importantly, dividing communities. The mixture of pork, politics, and power really does damage the environment, erode democracy, compromise peoples' organisations, discredit parts of our civil service, and divide and disrupt rural communities.

But citizens are fighting back and taking control again. In Manitoba, as in other places across this country and in the United States, we are winning this political battle at a local level. In the municipal elections in Manitoba in October of 2002, at least 30 people were elected who have been active in questioning and opposing mega-barns. We know of at least two municipal councils where mega-barn opponents have majority control.

The industry, suspecting that they were not going to do well politically, ran off to the province, and asked the government to take control of the situation. We want some "predictability" and "consistency," said the pork industry. Now, "predictability" and "consistency" are code words designed to obscure moves to take democratic control away from the people. The Province of Manitoba has announced that it intends, sometime in 2004, to take the democratic control away from local citizens by forcing the municipalities to adopt livestock bylaws that conform to provincial standards. Once this is done, a proponent will be able to locate a barn as close as 656 feet from any single residence and locate a lagoon as close as one mile from a community.

But the province and the industry will not succeed in suppressing the people. I've been chair of HogWatch Manitoba for three years. I've travelled around the whole province, and I've met people down in Piney, up the western side of the province in Angusville and Russell, and all over the province. And I am convinced of the strength of those people and those communities.

I was at a town hall meeting in March 2002 in Swan Lake. And there was a young farm woman there who had never been involved in issues before. Her name was Colleen Theissen. A barn was to be built near to her home and she said, "I'm downwind, I'm downhill, I'm downstream, and I'm damned mad!" She had organized the meeting and she was going to be on the panel and she was very nervous. And yet when it came time for her to make her presentation, I have never heard anybody speak so eloquently.

She talked about the struggle of agriculture, and about the constant struggle for people to survive in an economy that is so heavily weighted against them, and about the environmental factors that can also make it difficult for us. And she talked about three families. She traced the history of the first family back for 100 years, and she gave a brief description of the land they had occupied and what they had done. And she said their descendants were at that meeting that night. And she asked them to stand up. And they stood up and were recognized. She did the same for the two other families and they stood up. Then she concluded her remarks and asked, "Is it not time for the rest of you to stand up?" And they did. For me, that is what this struggle is about: It's about us standing up. This is our place. We are so old-fashioned in our thinking, we believe that we should have a say, as citizens, in constructing an economy that serves the needs of our community. We have no responsibility here to serve the needs of corporate investors who want to build hog barns. That is not our mandate.

We have to stand up to a destructive ideology that is destroying rural communities. The very ideology that destroyed the Crow Rate and took that economic benefit away from farmers, the very ideology that tore up the branch lines, the ideology that demolished the rural elevators, the ideology that stripped every bit of wealth from the prairies and left so much despair and waste: that ideology and its advocates now claim that they will save us by giving us hog megabarns. No thanks. They've done enough for us already. From this point on, we stand up. We take control. May the struggle continue.

This text is based on two speeches by Fred Tait: one at the Second Annual National Conference on Intensive Livestock Operations: Beyond Factory Farms (November 9, 2002); and the Second at the 33rd Annual

National Convention of the National Farmers Union (November 23, 2002); both in Saskatoon, Saskatchewan.

References

Bell, I. (2001, July 6). Minister reverses on marketing monopoly. *Western Producer.*

Chambers, A. (n.d.). Licensing of the Maple Leaf facilities in Brandon. *Manitoba Naturalists Society* [On-line]. Available: http://www.edcanada.org/map/maple.html)

Fallding, H. (2001, February 11). Tempers flare over hog fracas: Marketing board issue heats up NDP Convention. *Winnipeg Free Press*, p. A3.

Patton, W. (n.d.). *The Hudson Bay drainage system: Argument for a Canadian national water quality policy*. Available: www.sfu.ca/cstudies/science/water/pdf/Water-Ch05.pdf).

Chapter 4
The American Meat Factory
by Rick Dove

I have lived on the shores of the Neuse River near New Bern, North Carolina, for over 25 years. In 1987, after retiring as a Colonel in the United States Marine Corps, I pursued a childhood dream and became a commercial fisher. With three boats and a local seafood outlet store, my son Todd and I worked over 600 crab pots and more than 2,000 feet of gill nets. Things went well for the first two years. Then the fish began to die, many with open bleeding sores. At first it was only a few but, as time passed, the numbers grew larger and larger. Soon my son and I began to develop the same kind of sores on our legs, arms, and hands. It took months for these sores to heal. I also experienced memory loss. At the time I did not connect my son's and my health problems to our work on the water—that connection was established later.

By 1990, the situation became much worse. More and more of the fish in the Neuse River were developing bleeding lesions. Regrettably, my son Todd and I had no choice but to stop fishing. Frustrated and disappointed, I grudgingly returned to practising law. In 1991, the Neuse suffered the largest fish kill ever recorded in the state's history. Over one billion fish died over a period of six weeks during September and October. There were so many dead fish that some had to be bulldozed into the ground. Others were left to rot on the shore and river bottom. The stench produced by this kill was overwhelming and will never be forgotten.

In 1993, I became the Neuse Riverkeeper. In that capacity, I was a full-time paid citizen representative of the non-profit Neuse River Foundation whose duty it was to restore, protect, and enhance the waters of the 6,100-square-mile Neuse River watershed. Due to ill health attributed in large measure from my exposure to the toxins in the river, my work as Neuse Riverkeeper ended in July 2000. A short biographical outline together with a detailed description of the Neuse Riverkeeper Program can be found at www.riverkeeper.org.

As the Neuse Riverkeeper, I was in a position to study the river, to work with scientists and state officials, and to closely monitor the various sources of pollution. I patrolled the river by boat, aircraft, vehicle, and waders along with a corps of approximately 300 volunteers. All sources of pollution were exhaustively documented in thousands of photographs and hundreds of hours of video. By the time the next major fish fill occurred in 1995, I was in the best position to observe, report, and document the cause and effect of one of the river's most serious problems: nutrient pollution.

In the 1995 fish kill, for over 100 days, fish were once again dying in large numbers. Nearly all of them were covered with open bleeding lesions. In just 10 of those 100 days, volunteers working with the Neuse River Foundation documented more than 10,000,000 dead fish. At that time, many citizens who were exposed to this fish kill complained about a number of neurological and respiratory problems. North Carolina health authorities documented these problems and wrongly dismissed them. Later, researchers working similar fish kills on Maryland's Pokomoke River would link these same symptoms to the cause of the fish kills, *Pfiesteria piscicida*.

By 1995, we knew what was killing the fish. It was *Pfiesteria piscicida*, a one-celled animal, so tiny 100,000 of them would fit on the head of a pin. This creature, often referred to as the "cell from hell," produces an extremely powerful neurotoxin that paralyzes the fish, sloughs their skin, and eats their blood cells. It is capable of doing the same thing to humans. This neurotoxin is volatized to the air and is known to cause serious health problems, including memory loss, in humans who breathe it. Its proliferation has been directly linked to nutrient pollution from concentrated animal feeding operations (CAFOs), as well as other sources. One of the most exhaustive websites related to *Pfiesteria piscicida* can be found at www.pfiesteria.com.

The fish kills continue today. Depending upon weather conditions, some years are worse than others. Many smaller kills are not even counted. Fishers continue to report neurological and respiratory symptoms, and a dark cloud still hangs over the state's environmental reputation and economy.

From an office located in North Carolina, I now serve as the Southeastern Representative of Waterkeeper Alliance. The Alliance's headquarters is located in White Plains, New York. A major part of my duties involves assisting other Waterkeepers and investigating and documenting the environmental degradation resulting from CAFO operations, especially those involving hogs. The background on the Waterkeeper Alliance is set forth at www.keeper.org.

Introductions to the American Meat Factory

American meat production is currently undergoing the most dramatic consolidation in our history. Family farmers are disappearing and ceding control of the American landscapes and food production to industrial meat factories owned by a handful of giant corporations with little or no interest in or capacity for socially responsible agriculture.

Meat factories do not produce meat more efficiently than traditional family farmers. The industry's willingness to treat the animals with unspeakable cruelty and to dump thousands of tons of toxic pollutants into our nation's waterways, *and their ability to get away with it*, however, has given it a dramatic market advantage over the traditional family farm. Indeed, the industry's business plan is based upon its ability to use its political clout to paralyze the regulatory agencies, thereby escaping the true costs of producing its product.

For a decade, the Neuse Foundation and its Riverkeeper Program have been the leading voice against industrial hog production in North Carolina and one of the nation's leading repositories for information on industrial meat production. In December of 2000, Waterkeeper Alliance launched a national campaign designed to reform this industry and to restore healthy wholesome landscapes and waterways and bring back humanity, prosperity, and democracy to America's rural communities. The Alliance is partnering with animal welfare advocates, family farm advocates, other environmental groups, and others concerned about rural life in America to fight hog factories in the courts, at all levels of legislative decision-making and before the public. The Alliance has also created an elite legal team of attorneys from 15 prominent class action law firms who will use the courts to challenge the industry's control of America's rural landscapes and waterways. In February 2001, Waterkeeper staff attorneys and the legal team simultaneously filed a series of lawsuits against the industry in federal and state courts across the nation.

Industrial Pork Factories: A Threat to the Economy, the Environment, and Our Democracy

Industrial animal factories, invented in North Carolina, now threaten to extinguish family farming in 34 states.

In the late 1980s, a North Carolina state senator, Wendell Murphy, and his partners, Smithfield slaughterhouses, helped invent a new way to produce pork. Thousands of genetically enhanced hogs would be shoehorned into pens and tiny cages in giant metal warehouses, dosed with subtherapeutic antibiotics, and force-fed growth enhancers in their imported feeds. Their prodigious waste would be dumped, sprayed, spilled, and discharged onto adjacent landscapes and waterways. Within a few years, traditional North Carolina style hog farming gave way to the state's infamous pork factories mostly owned by a single corporation. In 1983, there were approximately 24,000 hog farms in North Carolina. Today, traditional family hog farmers are virtually extinct in North Carolina, replaced by 2,200 hog factories, 1,600 owned and/or controlled by Smithfield Foods Inc. Pork factories owned by Smithfield and a tiny handful of other large corporations, known as integrators, have now moved into 34 states and are affecting the most dramatic consolidation in United States agricultural history. The nation's largest 50 pork producers now control the vast majority of U.S. pork production. The largest producer, Smithfield Foods, controls over 24%, followed by Premium Standard Farms (7%), Seaboard Farms (6%), Prestage

Farms (4%), The Pork Group-Tyson (4%), Cargill (4%), Iowa Select Farms (3%), Christensen Farms (3%), and Purina Mills (2%).

By gaining control of every aspect of pork production from feed for baby pigs, to slaughterhouse packaging plants, to rendering facilities and transportation, Smithfield and other industrial producers were able to drive down the price of pork—through overproduction—and drive independent family farmers out of business while making up their own losses through greater profits at their slaughterhouses and packing plants. Proliferating pork factories have caused the number of hogs in North Carolina to soar from a few million in the mid-1980s to more than 10 million today, with most of this growth concentrated in North Carolina's sensitive coastal plain. During the same period, nearly 75% of North Carolina's family farmers were replaced by low-paying jobs in Smithfield's pork factories. By late 1998, pork prices to farmers dropped as low as 10 cents per pound at a time when the feed cost of raising a pig was 30 cents per pound. Adjusted for inflation, farmers were getting less for their hogs than during the Great Depression. The American consumer never saw the benefits of this extraordinary price reduction. Pork prices in the grocery stores remained stable. The industrial producers, most notably Smithfield, pocketed the profits at the slaughterhouses and thousands more family farmers went out of business.

The same process of vertical integration has bankrupted five out of six of America's hog farmers over the past 15 years and hammered a strong nail into the coffin of Thomas Jefferson's vision of a democracy rooted in family-owned freeholds. Approximately 70% of the swine raised in North Carolina are under Smithfield's ownership, with an even higher percentage among the hog factories in North Carolina's fragile coastal flood plain, including the Cape Fear, Neuse, and New River basins.

While hog barons often argue that industrial farming brings economic benefits to rural communities, the reality is the opposite. A mounting body of evidence proves that hog factories are bad for local economies and property values. Pork factories also cause a net loss of jobs. By machine-feeding hogs and keeping them continually confined, the pork barons have eliminated the need for animal husbandry. As few as two workers may tend a factory of 8,800 hogs. Each hog factory displaces three times as many jobs as it creates, replacing quality livelihoods with low-wage jobs for itinerant workers.

What has happened to traditional hog farming is also happening to other areas of meat production. North Carolina also produces over 700,000,000 chickens and 40,000,000 turkeys in much the same way as it produces hogs—factory style. This shift from traditional family farming to industrial production (CAFOs) is now taking place across America.

A tradition of land stewardship and animal husbandry is disappearing with the American family farmer.

In the 1980s, the majority of pork production was still in the hands of efficient independent farmers who kept herds small enough that they could provide husbandry to the animals, and the herd's manure production did not exceed fertilizer demand. The independent family farmer generally spreads the manure of a few hundred hogs as fertilizer on the same cropland from which he derives produce to feed his herd. Traditional farmers thus achieve a rough balance; growing crops that assimilate the nutrients in hog waste keeps these nutrients from flowing into adjacent waterways and leaching into groundwater. Recognizing that these practices benefit the public, Congress exempted the relatively small amounts of agricultural fertilizer that washed off farm fields into waterbodies from the Clean Water Act, Resource Conservation and Recovery Act (RCRA), and other environmental statutes.

By contrast, industrial hog producers confine thousands of animals in warehouses that produce tons of animal waste, liquefy that waste in open pits adjacent to the hog confinement areas, and spray massive quantities of the liquefied manure onto fields too small to absorb the nutrients. Poison runoff from these fields destroys the public waters that drain them. Smithfield hog factories quickly triumphed over family farmers in the marketplace, not due to their greater efficiency, but because the company adopted the dual strategies of vertical integration and of circumventing environmental and anti-cruelty laws. Hog producers reap enormous benefits by escaping the costs of waste disposal and proper animal husbandry, and, in effect, transferring these costs onto society.

Industrial pork production subjects millions of animals to conditions that are unspeakably and unnecessarily cruel.

Factory meat production is an industrial rather than an agricultural enterprise. Animal husbandry is nonexistent. Industrial pork barons produce pork chops and bacon and the animals themselves are treated only as industrial production units. Genetic manipulation for meat production has produced hog breeds that are high strung and nervous. They live short miserable lives characterized by extreme cruelty and extreme terror.

By nature, pigs are active, inquisitive, and intelligent, and they spend much of their time exploring ground cover and rooting for food. They are communal animals with a highly developed system of vocalization that they use in courtship, self-defense, and raising their young. The female pig, the sow, has a strong instinct to build a nest before giving birth. She will nurse her young for several months and take care of them even longer.

In industrialized hog factories, pigs are raised in intensive confinement for their entire lives in huge windowless structures, choked by their own foul stenches. Subject to disease from overcrowding and entirely deprived of exercise, sunlight, straw bedding, rooting opportunities, and social interactions that are fundamental to their health, factory hogs are kept healthy only by constant doses of subtherapeutic antibiotics. Their growth rates are unnaturally sped-up by feed additives including antibiotics, hormones, and toxic metals. Sows endure tiny crates that are too small for them to turn around, giving birth on bare metal grate floors, their babies taken away after only three weeks of nursing. Driven by frustration and depression, sows continually gnaw on the metal bars of their crates. Severe restrictions on the pigs' movement over a lifetime impede bone development frequently resulting in broken legs. Injured pigs are "culled" sometimes by being dumped alive into waste lagoons. There are many accounts of brutal treatment of these animals, including teeth pulling, castration without anesthesia, and beating disabled sows unable or too terror-stricken to walk to slaughter. According to the U.S. Humane Society, *one in five of all factory-raised pigs die prematurely*, before reaching the slaughterhouse.

In 1999, Smithfield made a major foray into Poland. At the invitation of the Animal Welfare Institute, Andrzej Lepper, the president of Poland's largest farmers' union, came to the United States and toured Smithfield hog factories. Mr. Lepper later recounted that he was shocked by what he saw in the American hog factories which he referred to as "animal concentration camps." He added that "industrial husbandry methods of raising hogs are not in harmony with nature."

The Catholic Church catechism holds that it is legitimate for humans to raise animals for food, but also says that it is "contrary to human dignity to cause animals to suffer or die needlessly." In December 2000, a Vatican official wrote that factory livestock operations, with their cramped and cruel methods, may cross the line of morally acceptable treatment of animals.

Pollution-based profits.

Industrial hog factories cram thousands of hogs into pens and cages for a lifetime over slatted concrete and metal grate floors. Whereas traditional independent farmers raised their hogs on pasture or straw bedding which captured the manure, controlled odours, and was spread regularly onto crops as fertilizer, factory pork producers completely deprive their hogs of straw bedding so that they can liquefy the waste, which increases odours and leads to runoff. Their waste falls though the floor to a cellar below the buildings that the operators periodically flush into an open-air earthen pit, euphemistically referred to as a "lagoon." In North Carolina, flushing liquid comes from the lagoons. These manure pits are really putrid cesspools one to 20 acres in size and up to 15 feet deep, brimming with tens of millions of gallons of untreated feces, urine, and toxic waste generally destined to ooze its way onto soils and into subsurface waters and rivers.

Using a variety of water cannons, hog factories spray this *raw urine and fecal marinade* from their waste pits onto adjacent land, ostensibly as fertilizer. Industrial hog factories illegally deposit hundreds of millions of pounds of untreated hog feces and urine and other contaminants into the sprayfields each year. However, the frightening tonnage of liquid and solid hog excreta generated by swine cities vastly exceeds the absorption capacity of the crops on sprayfields for nitrogen, phosphorous, and metals. Most sprayfields are heavily ditched to carry subsurface and surface runoff directly to public waters.

These discharges overload public waterways with nutrients, injuring aquatic life and endangering human health. According to the federal Environmental Protection Agency (EPA), 60% of river miles, 50% of lake access, and 34% of estuary acres are degraded by agricultural pollution, mostly from factory farms. In addition to nutrients, swine waste lagoons contain a witch's brew of nearly 400 volatile organic compounds and toxic poisons including pathogenic microbes (protozoas, bacteria, viruses), biocides, pesticides, disinfectants, food additives, salts, heavy metals (especially zinc and copper), antibiotics, hormones, and other materials.

Industrial pork producers' primary economic advantage has been their ability to have the public subsidize their waste disposal. A single hog can produce 10 times the fecal waste and four-and-a-half times the nitrogen produced by a human being. A hog factory with 100,000 hogs can produce fecal waste loads equivalent to a city of one million people. One facility planned for the Rosebud Sioux Reservation in South Dakota will house 860,000 hogs and produce more waste than New York City! According to a formula developed by Professor Mark Sobsey, University of North Carolina, School of Public Health (Chapel Hill), in *North Carolina's environmentally sensitive coastal plain (area between the coast and I-95) hogs produce more fecal waste on a daily basis than that produced by all the people combined in the states of North Carolina, California, New York, Pennsylvania, New Hampshire, North Dakota, and Texas.* While human waste must be treated at sewer plants or in septic systems, industrial pork producers simply dump thousands of tons of equally virulent and far more concentrated hog waste onto lands and into waters.

If hog factories were to construct sewer plants for each of their pork factories, as cities are required to do for human waste, it would raise production costs by upwards of $170 per hog. This is the equivalent of over 60 cents per pound at kill weight, a price that would destroy the industry's market dominance. Alternative treatment technologies, all of them less effective than conventional sewage treatment, would still raise production costs high above market levels.

Antibiotic use promotes resistant bacteria.

Industrial meat producers routinely dose their animals with sub-therapeutic antibiotics for non-medical purposes, primarily to stimulate unnaturally rapid growth in hogs. The excessive use of antibiotics is an integral part of the production system, both to bring them to market faster and to keep them alive in otherwise unliveable conditions. Many of the antibiotics given to livestock, such as tetracycline, penicillin, and erythromycin, are important human medicines. Up to 80% of antibiotics administered to hogs pass unchanged through the animal to bacteria-rich waste lagoons. This soup is then spread on sprayfields, allowing the antibiotics to enter groundwater and run off into surface waters.

Routine administration of sub-therapeutic antibiotics endangers public health by contributing to drug-resistant pathogens with which humans and animals may come in contact through ground water, surface water, soil, air, or food products. Once antibiotics have entered hog factory effluents, they can enter waterways and spread through the environment in low concentrations—killing susceptible bacteria and leaving resistant survivors to multiply. Resistant bacteria can then infect people who swim in lakes and rivers or drink well water.

In January 2001, the Union of Concerned Scientists issued a report that included the following shocking statistic: *84% of all antibiotics consumed are used in livestock, the vast majority for nontherapeutic purposes!* The hog industry uses 11 million pounds of antibiotics annually, while a comparatively modest three million pounds are used in human medicine.

Many public health officials have warned that the use of subtherapeutic antibiotics in hogs is extremely dangerous. The World Health Organization, the U.S. Centers for Disease Control and Prevention, and the American Public Health Association have all urged that using the antibiotics of human medicine in hogs should be prohibited. The European Union has banned nontherapeutic agricultural use of antibiotics that are important in human medicine. In some European countries, such as Sweden, using any antibiotics in raising hogs is illegal.

Alternatives.

There is a myriad of alternatives to the lagoon and sprayfield system, but the industrial hog barons refuse to adopt innovations that might cut profit margins. For example, in Sweden, where factory farming is banned, hogs are raised in a deep-bedded straw system, where ample straw bedding is provided to pigs who are allowed to move freely, interact socially with other pigs, and engage in other natural behaviours such as rooting and nest building. There are no farrowing crates. There is no liquefied manure, no waste pits, and none of the stench that envelops the American hog factories. Under the Swedish system, there is little risk of environmental injury because the manure is not liquefied and is naturally composted in the straw. Pigs raised under these conditions are also unstressed and healthier. The animals in Swedish farms and the people who raise them exist in a much healthier environment because they emit substantially less pollution to the air. In America, a number of family farmers still use improved traditional methods to produce vegetables, meat, and milk. Organic Valley and Niman Ranch are two successful leaders in this field. Their products are wholesome and tasty and they are produced through sustainable farming methods. Where animals are involved, they are treated humanely. These farmers do not use growth hormones or subtherapeutic antibiotics, and their farming practices are environmentally sound. These farmers could easily out-compete their industrial competitors if the industrialists were required to bear the full cost of protecting the environment.

Hog barons proliferate through a pattern of law-breaking.

By illegally polluting, industrial hog producers gained a critical advantage over their competitors—the American family farmers—in the marketplace. These are not business people making an "honest buck." Instead, they are law-breakers and bullies who can only make money by polluting our air and water and violating the laws with which other Americans must comply.

Environmental law-breaking is an integral component of factory pork production. Records of state environmental agencies in over a dozen states demonstrate that factory hog producers are chronic violators of state and federal law. Smithfield's corrupt institutional culture and business practices are not restricted to North Carolina. In 1985, the Chief Justice of the Fourth U.S. Circuit Court of Appeals upheld the largest civil penalty ever imposed under the "citizen suit" provisions of the federal Clean Water Act, $1,285,322, against Smithfield for polluting the Pagan River in Smithfield's home state of Virginia. A 1996 23-count Federal indictment from Virginia charged a Smithfield manager and operator with both falsifying and destroying sampling records and intentional illegal discharges of toxic wastewater into the Pagan River. These actions resulted in an 18-month prison sentence and a record $12.6 million civil penalty assessed by the U.S. District Court in 1997. Virginia recently charged Smithfield with more than 22,000 pollution violations from the mid-1980s to the mid-1990s. This case was dismissed in March 2001 by a judge who said that the federal action preempted the state's claims (based on *res judicata*).

Also, North Carolina's Department of Environment and Natural Resources (NCDENR) records show thousands of violations by Smithfield's facilities of state environmental laws. This is notable considering North Carolina's lack of inspectors and extremely poor enforcement record. The number of violations is believed to be considerably greater since, prior to 1995, the environmental agency was not even allowed to know the locations of the hog factories, or to inspect them unless "invited" to do so by the operators or owners. Needless to say, such "invitations" were exceedingly rare. The massive and persistent drumbeat of violations recorded in these documents prove that hog factories and their facilities are chronic, deliberate, and habitual violators of state laws designed to protect the environment and minimize discharges of swine waste. The State of North Carolina requires that hog facilities adhere to a Certified Animal Waste Management Plan designed to keep animal wastes and other pollutants confined to the facility so they will not be released into public waterways. Records kept by the NCDENR Division of Water Quality (DWQ) and assembled by North Carolina Sierra Club show that Smithfield's pork factories regularly, habitually, persistently, and dependably violate their certified waste plans or operate illegally without the required National Pollutant Discharge Elimination System (NPDES) permits.

Indeed, without breaking the law, pork factories cannot make money and produce hogs as efficiently or cheaply as family farmers. Industrial pork producers instead rely on rare inspections and small fines by state regulators. The rare penalties and small dollar amounts occasionally dispensed by state enforcers never provide sufficient incentive for the industrial pork barons to stop their law-breaking. These fines amount only to a trivial cost of doing business.

The industry locates its facilities in rural states where they can easily dominate the political landscapes. Weak state agencies are the primary consideration in siting the industry's new facilities. A 1998 study found clear evidence that the *level of enforcement* of environmental laws and regulations, even more than their stringency, had a direct influence on the growth of the hog industry (Mo & Abdalla, 1998). The more lenient a state's enforcement program, the more likely it is to see growth in the hog industry. Hog factories also tend to locate in minority communities where opposition is considered by the industry to be more easily silenced.

Waterkeeper Alliance Campaign against Industrialized Hog Factories

Waterkeeper's Hog Factory Campaign.

The consolidation of pork production by large industries and the proliferation of pork factories with lagoons and sprayfields have caused a dramatic public reaction in farm states particularly among factory neighbours. Many citizen organizations mobilized in the late 1980s to oppose the proliferation of meat factories. These groups began attending meetings of local boards of health, county commissions, and drain commissions, and voicing their concerns to state and federal legislative bodies and agencies. Farmers, fishers, and property owners warned the industry that its public claims that these factories could operate without polluting the air and waterways would be exposed as false. Corporate pork production has harmed so many people in different ways that many groups have identified it as a threat to their constituencies. By the early 1990s, watchdog organizations such as the Waterkeeper Alliance (through its local Riverkeeper programs) have been raising concerns and exposing chronic and severe violations of environmental laws.

Waterkeeper's legal campaign.

The Waterkeeper organizations have a strong track record of bringing legal actions against polluters to enforce environmental laws. Waterkeeper Alliance president Robert F. Kennedy, Jr. founded the Alliance and co-directs the Environmental Litigation Clinic at Pace University School of Law, which is known for its groundbreaking work in environmental enforcement. Waterkeeper has also assembled an élite team of nationally recognized class action law firms to address pollution and health problems caused by the hog industry. Waterkeeper is coordinating a national legal attack designed to civilize the factory pork industry through a series of lawsuits and administrative actions under federal environmental laws, state "nuisance" and health laws, and the federal racketeering law (RICO).

In December 2000, Waterkeeper Alliance issued Letters of Intent to Sue to six industrial hog facilities impacting the Neuse, New, and Cape Fear rivers in North Carolina for violations of the Clean Water Act, Resource Conservation and Recovery Act (RCRA), and Comprehensive Environmental Response, Compensation, and Liability Act (CERCLA). Waterkeeper subsequently filed lawsuits under environmental statutes against two Smithfield-owned hog factories in North Carolina and is engaged in settlement discussions with others. Waterkeeper Alliance is working with environmental and farm organizations and activists in Michigan, Minnesota, Iowa, and South Dakota to develop other lawsuits to reform the hog industry in each of those states.

In June of 2000, the Alliance and the North Carolina Riverkeeper organizations filed a 36-count lawsuit in North Carolina Superior Court against all of Smithfield's North Carolina operations. Invoking the state's nuisance laws and the public trust doctrine, the suit seeks an order requiring that the hog factories stop polluting local waterways and the air and redress the damage they have caused to North Carolina's rivers and river communities.

Finally, Waterkeeper is assisting grass-root activists in defending themselves against industry lawsuits to intimidate them from exercising their constitutional rights to petition and to free expression. For example, Waterkeeper's attorneys are currently fighting a so-called SLAPP (Strategic Lawsuit Against Public Participation) suit against a group of Nebraska farmers by Sands, Nebraska's largest industrial hog producer. Sands filed the suit in an attempt to harass farmers who had filed comments with the Nebraska Department of Environmental Quality regarding an application by Sands to significantly expand one of its facilities without appropriate environmental safeguards. Sands is suing for defamation and emotional distress. The outcome of this case could be crucial to the future of public participation in industrial meat factory issues. Waterkeeper attorneys have filed a counterclaim against Sands claiming that the industry lawsuit violates Nebraska's anti-SLAPP statute and is a lawsuit intended to silence the community's right to freely express its opposition to this industry.

The Federal Government Steps in, then Bush Administration Backs Off

Although the Clean Water Act, adopted 30 years ago, explicitly recognizes Concentrated Animal Feeding Operations (CAFOs) as a major threat to water quality by enumerating them as a regulated point source, neither the federal EPA nor the state agencies have fully implemented a Clean Water Act permitting program for CAFOs. In fact, some states, such as North Carolina and Michigan, vehemently denied for years that they were required to establish a Clean Water Act CAFO permitting program.

The failure of the states and the federal government to implement the Clean Water Act and enforce existing laws and regulations against CAFOs has resulted in the widespread violation of the statute and its regulations by the livestock and poultry industries. *This widespread violation of the Clean Water Act is acknowledged by EPA itself and the livestock industry (CAFO NODA, p. 58571), which is now ironically using its failure to comply with existing regulations as an excuse for its inability to bear the cost of proposed, more stringent regulations. They represent a violation of the statutory mandate of EPA to develop regulations for this industry that use the best available technology, a standard that does not permit EPA to disregard an existing technology because it is more expensive for industry.* This universal failure to implement the nation's most important water protection legislation is a national scandal and has resulted in a substantial degradation of our nation's waters due to agricultural pollution.

In recognition of the environmental destruction that large livestock and poultry operations have been wreaking on the environment and because it was sued by NRDC, EPA published proposed new regulations for CAFOs and NPDES permitting guidelines on January 12, 2001. In March 2001, representatives of the major livestock and poultry producers petitioned the Bush administration for an extension of the comment deadline, so the Administration pushed the comment deadline back to July 30, 2001.

Following submission of public comments on the proposed regulations, EPA published a Notice of Date Availability; National Pollutant discharge Elimination System Permit Regulations; and Effluent Guidelines and Standards for Concentrated Animal Feeding Operations (referred to herein as "the November 12 regulations" or "the NODA"). (Federal Register Vol.66, No.225, 58556, Nov 21, 2001.) The NODA states that the January 12 regulations generated a significant number of comments from livestock and poultry industry representatives or land grant university professors who argued that EPA had failed to adequately calculate the costs and/or economic impact. Section V, pages 58566-58591, is devoted entirely to financial and economic analysis.

Reading through the November 12 regulations, one might have guessed that "EPA" stands for "*Economic* Protection Agency." The NODA seeks input on approximately 88 different issues, the majority of which request comments related to cost and economic or financial impact. Virtually every revision proposes a weaker regulation than the earlier version. In fact, in no case does the November 12 version propose a stricter environmental standard.

While the January 12 CAFO regulations moved EPA in the direction of solving some of the ills caused by CAFOs, the November 12 regulations suggest substantially scaling back these efforts and demonstrate a deterioration of the federal government's only serious attempt to address the crescendo of citizen and scientific voices in this country calling for major CAFO reform.

The November 12 regulations are an alarming retreat by the federal EPA from the January 12, 2001 version of the regulations. It is troubling that, at the moment in history when the public outcry over CAFO pollution is the loudest, EPA signals its withdrawal from its earlier commitment to address it and finally to require this industry to comply with the Clean Water Act. The January 12 version, the result of years of EPA, citizen, and industry review and dialogue, was crafted to make necessary improvements in the regulation of CAFOs. The November 12 regulations have many shortcomings. They—

1. fail to consider cost to environment;
2. fail to consider whether an operation is a family farm;

3. would allow states to avoid implementing the Clean Water Act;
4. move toward fewer NPDES permits;
5. reduce critical groundwater protection;
6. propose inappropriate Phosphorous "banking;"
7. propose less frequent manure sampling;
8. allow inappropriate exception for a "chronic storm event;"
9. allow non-compliance to be a boon to violators;
10. would allow the inappropriate substitution of Environmental Management Systems (EMS) for compliance with Clean Water Act and CAFO regulations;
11. contain a faulty definition of "Proper Agricultural Practice;"
12. propose an inappropriate substitution of co-permitting by Environmental Management Systems (EMS); and
13. attempt to circumvent the plain language or intent of the Clean Water Act.

Conclusion

Over the past 30 years we have seen some of the most popular and effective environmental laws ever enacted in the history of the U.S. The creation of the Environmental Protection Agency and the Clean Water, Clean Air, and Resource Conservation and Recovery Acts improved our rivers, streams, and groundwater as well as the air we breathe. These laws and regulations, while not yet fully implemented, have helped protect our forests, parks, and wildlife. As a direct result, the quality of life in America has substantially improved. Clearly, this period has been one of the most progressive and prosperous in our nation's history.

There have been periods of darkness as well. The U.S. environment and its dependent economy were under heavy assault during the 104th Congress. Fortunately, under the strong leadership of President Clinton and his administration, America weathered that storm. Now our environment and economy are once again being placed in serious jeopardy. The environmental laws and regulations that promoted the strong economy of the 1990s are being attacked once again, this time not by a wayward Congress but by a President out of touch with the importance of a healthy environment—a President and an administration blinded by corporate interests.

President Bush's disregard of the nexus between good environmental policies and a healthy economy is not surprising. His record in Texas predicted it. While anti-environmental statements did not flow from his lips during the presidential campaign, actions immediately following his oath of office gave clear warning of what was in store.

Through his Chief-of-Staff, President Bush issued a directive that prevents a series of Clinton environmental actions from taking place. The directive imposed a moratorium that effectively prevented any new rules from being printed in the Federal Register until they were specifically approved by the administration. That blocked most of Clinton's executive orders. These directives specifically targeted environmental restrictions on runoff from animal feeding operations. President Bush also proclaimed that many older regulations would be actively reviewed and possibly rescinded.

While America's attention has been focused on the war against terrorism, President Bush has been quietly unraveling federal rules established to implement the environmental laws of our country and to safeguard our natural resources. We once again risk corporations who profit from pollution gaining the upper hand. The progress we made, and from which we economically benefited, over the past 30 years is fading fast.

Specifically, after the terrorist attacks on September 11, the Bush administration began to intensify its effort to turn back the environmental clock by gutting old and new environmental rules and regulations. With the nation focused on the war, the Bush administration weakened Clean Air and Water initiatives and enforcement, weakened wetland protections, gave a green light to pollution-based mining activities, blocked rules that would minimize raw sewage discharges into waterways, and gave new power to the Office of Management and Budget (OMB) to weaken and tie up existing environmental rules.

The citizens of the United States need and deserve protection from the environmental and health dangers posed by CAFOs and the industry giants who control them. The EPA must focus on the protection of the environment, not protection of the livestock industry.

Although they failed to do everything necessary to solve the environmental and health problems from CAFOs, EPA's January 12 regulations were a step in the right direction. Unfortunately, EPA's November 12 CAFO regulations propose to diminish even these improvements.

The EPA must refocus its efforts on promulgating CAFO regulations that will fully protect the environment which is the house in which we live. The Congress should see to it that the President lives up to his responsibilities to protect our environment, which in turn protects our national heritage and national security.

References

Mo & Abdalla. (1998, June 7). Analysis finds swine expansion driven most by economic factors, local decisions. *Feedstuffs*.

Chapter 5
The Smell of Intensive Pig Production on the Canadian Prairies

by Bill Paton

Odour complaints are one of the most significant public issues for today's confined livestock and poultry industries. Most problems arise with intensive pig and poultry units, while there are relatively few long-term odour difficulties with dairy cows or beef units. Significant problems also arise when animal manures are stored for lengthy periods.

Odours have recently become a major challenge for the pork industry due to the trend on the Prairies toward intensive livestock operations (ILOs) in which large numbers of pigs are confined in small areas. Odours from pig barns are caused by rotting feed, dust and gas emissions, incineration of dead pigs and unprocessed pig carcasses, and by manure—particularly as it decomposes in the absence of oxygen.

Anaerobic (oxygen deprived) storage of manure, the most common practice in prairie swine production, is the worst choice as far as odours are concerned. Anaerobic microbial activity during manure slurry storage in underslat channels or lagoons results in the production of malodourous compounds. In contrast, in straw bedding hog barns the straw absorbs a large proportion of urine, and aerobic conditions tend to predominate. Excreta and straw provide the required ingredients for good compost and will produce well-rotted farmyard manure, which has a good traditional country smell.

The offensive smells from slurry storage structures are intensified under severe winter conditions when biological activity is minimized. Odours may also arise from land spreading of wastes, and odours from wastes are carried on dust and other particles as well as in gases and vapours.

"Nuisance" is defined as the presence of offensive smelling air at such an intensity, concentration, frequency, and duration as to materially interfere with the normal use and enjoyment of property. It is difficult to determine the impact area of odourous gas emissions because it continuously changes with wind speed and direction. Community tolerance to odours can be assessed by surveying residents in the surrounding neighbourhood while simultaneously monitoring weather and odour. Environmental odours can have a considerable impact upon a population's general well being, affecting both its physiological and psychological status.

The technology to completely prevent and remove odours either does not exist or is prohibitively expensive to install and/or manage. Initial site selection and facility location is absolutely critical for reducing nuisance odour complaints. Proper siting, design, and day-to-day management of waste activities to prevent odour formation is the preferred approach. Hog industry producers have a responsibility to ensure minimal impact on the surrounding area, including odour-related issues.

What Makes Liquid Hog Manure Smell

There may be over 300 kinds of substances that cause odour problems. They include the common inorganic odour-causing substances hydrogen sulfide (H2S) and ammonia (NH3). Landfills, livestock farms, hog manure, and wastewater treatment plants may give off a wide range of concentrations of H2S and NH3. These chemicals can be detected by smell at concentrations of 1.1 parts per billion by volume (ppbv) for H2S and 37 ppbv for NH3.

Taiwan has designated H2S and NH3 air pollutants for decades because of both their odour-causing properties and their adverse effects on human health when inhaled. H2S is a colourless gas that smells like rotten eggs. It is slightly denser than air, so it collects in low areas outdoors and near the floor indoors. It burns with a bluish flame, is very poisonous, and is both an irritant and asphyxiant. Olfactory nerve fatigue occurs rapidly, impairing the sense of smell so odour is not a reliable indicator of exposure. High concentrations of H2S have been reported in manure slurry pits. Even higher transient concentrations (up to 541 ppm) were found to be a feature of slatted floor systems.

In a British study, 168 different chemical species were identified in manure slurry odour. Of these, 30 have odour detection thresholds lower than or equal to 0.001mg/m3. Six of the 10 compounds with the lowest odour detection thresholds contained sulphur. Other researchers have identified a broad range of compounds in livestock manure including volatile organic acids, alcohols, aldehydes, amines, carbonyls, esters, sulfides, disulfides, mercaptans, and nitrogen heterocyclics.

Amine emissions have been studied because of their inherent toxicity and the potential carcinogenicity of their reaction products, particularly the nitrosamines. Trimethylamine (TMA) is the predominant amine emitted from animal wastes with smaller odour contributions from monomethylamine, isopropylamine, ethylamine, n-butylamine, and amylamine. Secondary amines, dimethylamine, and diethylamine have also been identified inside livestock houses.

The organic portion of manure consists of proteins, carbohydrates, and fats. Anaerobic decomposition degrades the proteins to ammonia, hydrogen sulphide, and short chain organic acids. The carbohydrates decompose to organic acids, which are further converted to alcohols, water, carbon dioxide, and hydrocarbons, especially methane. The fats degrade to fatty acids and alcohols, and the fatty acids in turn form water, carbon dioxide, and methane. The alcohols can undergo oxidation to aldehydes and ketones.

Ammonia may react with alcohols and organic acids to produce amines and amides. Hydrogen sulphide can react with alcohols and organic acids resulting in mercaptans and thioacids. Further reactions can produce disulphides. Bacterial metabolism of the inorganic portion of manure can also produce ammonia, hydrogen sulphide, and carbon dioxide.

Odours In The Vicinity Of Hog Barns

The odours emitted from an ILO are affected by the number, type, and weight of pigs, building design and management, techniques of manure handling, treatment, storage, and application, and odour control technology. Wind direction and velocity, humidity, topography, temperature, and unique meteorological conditions (such as temperature inversions) affect odour transport and direction.

Setback regulations may consist of fixed setbacks or setbacks that consider some site-specific information. For example the American Society of Agricultural Engineering Practice 379.1 Control of Manure Odors (ASAE, 1997) recommends 2.6 km (1 mile) from a housing development and 0.65 to 1.3 km (0.25 to 0.5 miles) from neighbouring residences.

Van Kleeck and Bulley conducted a survey of neighbours around seven, 100-to-225 sow farrow-to-finish operations in order to assess the relationship between the perception of odour nuisance, separation distance, and the size of the hog facility. The frequency of neighbours perceiving pig farms as a nuisance was inversely proportional to the square of the separation distance. About 20% of neighbours living around .67 km (2,200 feet) away from swine farms perceived them to be a nuisance. Farm size had no effect between .18 and .36 km (600 and 1200 feet) away. It is worth noting that this study examined operations that are much smaller than the ILOs currently being built and proposed in Canada today.

Many states, provinces, and countries have incorporated setbacks into their regulations that depend very roughly on animal type, land use, and/or size of facility ranging from .224 km (.14 miles) to unlimited.

Odour Affects Health In Many Ways

A number of studies show a direct relationship between non-toxicological odours and symptomology. Noxious environmental odours may trigger symptoms by physiological mechanisms such as exacerbation of underlying medical conditions, innate odour aversions, aversive conditioning phenomena, stress-induced illness, and possible pheromonal reactions.

Unpleasant odours can affect well-being by eliciting unpleasant sensations, triggering possible harmful reflexes, modifying olfactory function, and other physiological reactions. Annoyance and depression can result from exposure to unpleasant odours along with nausea, vomiting, headache, shallow breathing, coughing, sleep disturbances, and loss of appetite. Odourous compounds associated with livestock production that are at low concentrations but above odour thresholds are still likely to generate complaints.

In 1698 Sir John Floyer identified odours as factors that can worsen asthma, but this relationship is generally unappreciated by physicians. More recently others have reported the same observations with asthma patients.

A study in Finland examined the effects of very low-level exposure to malodourous sulfur compounds on eye irritation, respiratory-tract symptoms, and central nervous system symptoms in adults. The residents receiving the reduced sulphur compound odours reported an excess of coughs, respiratory infections, and headaches during the preceding 12-month period. These results indicated that adverse effects of malodourous sulphur compounds could occur at lower concentrations than previously reported.

A more recent study reports more tension, depression and anger, reduced vigour, and more confusion among the exposed group than a control population not exposed to odours from commercial swine operations. These findings are consistent with previous studies in which odours of varying properties have been found to affect mood. In other situations, odours have also been reported to affect cognitive performance and physiological responses including heart rate and electroencephalographic patterns.

A variety of factors may play a role in the altered mood of residents who are exposed to odours from nearby swine operations, including the unpleasantness of the sensory quality of the odour; the intermittent nature of the stimulus; learned aversions to the odour; potential neural stimulation of immune responses via direct neural connections between odour centres in the brain and lymphoid tissue; direct physical effects from molecules in the plume including nasal and respiratory irritation; possible chemo-sensory disorders; and unpleasant thoughts associated with the odour.

Experiencing Hog Manure Odour

At moderate to high odour intensities, most people rate the quality of the odour from intensive hog barns as unpleasant. The odour is not only perceived while breathing outdoor air but can also be perceived within homes of nearby residents due to air circulation through open windows and air conditioning systems. The odourant molecules can be absorbed by clothing, curtains, and building materials, which act as sinks. The molecules are then released slowly from the textiles and other materials over a period after the plume has passed, thus increasing the time residents are exposed to the air pollutants.

Conditioned aversions to odours are well documented in the scientific literature. Aversive conditioning can occur if environmental odours are associated with an irritant such as ammonia gas or other toxic chemicals such as pesticides. In addition, conditioned alterations in immune responses using smell and taste (chemosensory) stimuli provide strong evidence for functional relationships between chemosensory centres in the brain and the immune system. Both conditioned immuno-suppression and immuno-enhancement have been reported using chemosensory stimuli as the conditioned stimulus.

There is also a potential for unpleasant odours to influence physical health without the involvement of learning or conditioning due to the direct anatomical connections between the olfactory system and the immune system. Brain structures broadly involved in smell can modulate immune responses, especially via the integrated circuitry of the limbic cortex, limbic forebrain, hypothalamus, and brain stem. The links between the brain and the immune system are bidirectional so that immune responses can also affect odour centres in the brain.

Components in the odour plume may also have direct physical effects on the body. Indeed some of the odour-contributing molecules from hog farms can cause nasal and respiratory irritation. Nasal irritation has been shown to elevate adrenalin, which may contribute to feelings of anger and tension.

The volatile organic compounds (VOCs) responsible for odours may also be absorbed directly by the body (into the bloodstream and fat stores) via gas exchange in the lungs. Persons who have absorbed odourants through the lungs can sometimes smell the odour for hours after exposure due to slow release of the odourants from the bloodstream into expired air activating the olfactory receptors.

Volatile organic compounds are well known to be eliminated in breath after exposure. Persons with olfactory dysfunction caused by factors unrelated to swine odour such as concurrent medical conditions, drugs they are taking, or pesticide exposure, may find the odour even more objectionable due to their abnormal smell function.

Finally, odours may alter mood because they are associated with unpleasant thoughts. Some persons consider the stench from hog barns a taboo odour, which they should not have to endure. For others, the odours generate environmental concerns, fear of loss of use and value of property, or a conviction that odours interfere with their enjoyment of life and property. Part of the motivation for odour complaints may be increased awareness of other environmental agents, such as tobacco smoke, which are both malodourous and dangerous to one's health.

Health Effects of Hydrogen Sulphide Exposure

There is a significant body of research on the acute effects (short-term exposure to high levels) of hydrogen sulphide gas. Workers who are required to work in sewers and other workplace environments where hydrogen sulphide may be present are required to wear respiratory equipment. In Iowa, incidents are frequently reported in which someone is overcome by manure gases. These incidents have resulted in several deaths and many more illnesses caused by exposure to these poisonous gases. Deaths have occurred in recent years on pig farms in Manitoba. Workers in pig barns are not covered by Manitoba's Workplace Safety and Health regulations. Hog barns are also exempt from compulsory participation in workers' compensation programs.

The health consequences of chronic exposure (long-term exposure to low levels) to hydrogen sulphide have not been studied as much or for very long periods. There is little evidence of persistent or cumulative effects when exposure is kept below 20 ppm. At exposures above 20 ppm, the following have been recorded: fatigue; changes of personality, intellect, and memory; eye and respiratory irritation; gastrointestinal disorders; decreased libido; and backache.

Health Effects of Ammonia Exposure

Respiratory tract irritation, rhinitis, sinusitis, bronchitis, asthma, and odour related psychological symptoms are human sensitive determinants associated with hazardous chemicals generated in the intensive swine farming environment.

Among the prevalent swine farm gases and chemical species, ammonia is the primary irritant. Dose-related ammonia-induced inflammatory response has been observed in pigs exposed to ammonia up to 10,000 ppbv for six days in an air-pollutant exposure chamber. Exposure of fertilizer plant workers to chemicals such as urea, ammonia, and diammonium phosphate resulted in significant obstructive lung changes affecting the larger airways and bronchospasm after long periods of exposure.

Air samples collected at the breathing zone of farm workers in an Iowa pig farm from July to October 1995 showed the measured ammonia concentration outside the swine confinement building was 66 to 330 ppbv. A gradual increase in ammonia concentration in the vicinity of the barn was observed from summer to fall season. The highest indoor ammonia concentrations typically occurred during the fall to winter season (April, 1995—7,000 ppbv; November, 1995—10,000 ppbv). Comparatively, ammonia concentrations in the urban atmosphere typically range from 1 to 5 ppbv. This means that the ammonia concentration outside intensive hog production facilities is at least 10 to 60 times higher than the average ammonia levels reported in the urban and industrial metropolitan atmosphere. Ammonia concentration within the swine confinement facility was

250- to 750- times higher in the summer and more than 1,500- times greater than urban concentrations in the fall and spring seasons.

With increasing ventilation air flow, ammonia emissions in piggeries can increase. This is due to increased air movement around the manure surface, affecting the mass transfer coefficient of ammonia and also because ventilation air flow affects the difference in vapour pressure between ammonia in the manure and ammonia in the air.

Neighbouring Communities Exposed to Outdoor Air Pollution

An Iowa study assessing the physical and mental health of residents living in the vicinity of a large-scale swine confinement operation (4,000 sows) reported that neighbours experienced significantly higher rates of four clusters of symptoms known to represent toxic or inflammatory effects on the respiratory tract. These clusters of symptoms have been well documented among intensive hog barn workers.

Similar health problems have been identified among hog community residents in eastern North Carolina. Three rural communities were compared in this study, one in the vicinity of an approximately 6,000-head hog operation, one in the vicinity of two intensive cattle operations, and a third where residents lived at least two miles from livestock operations that use liquid waste management systems. Hog community residents reported increased occurrence of headaches, runny noses, sore throats, excessive coughing, diarrhea, and burning eyes compared to residents of the community with no close-by livestock operations. Quality of life, as indicated by the number of times residents could not open windows or go outside even in nice weather, was similar in control and cattle communities but greatly reduced among residents of the hog community.

Two field studies in two cities in Northrhine-Westfalia, Germany were carried out in order to characterize the degree of association between environmental odour exposure, annoyance, and somatic (physical) symptoms. In both studies, odour effects were assessed through personal interviews using standardized questionnaires. In the second study, the odour source was a pig-rearing facility, and the degree of odour exposure was assessed by measuring the frequency of odour events by means of systematic field observations.

Results showed that the degree of odour annoyance, as well as the frequency of somatic symptoms, increased significantly with increasing odour exposure. In both studies, perceived negative health was associated with increased symptom reports. The author concluded that environmental odours should be considered as a risk factor for the health and well being of exposed populations, especially for vulnerable individuals with poor health status.

Hog Workers Exposed to Indoor Air Pollution

A number of health problems have been found to be associated with veterinarians responsible for intensively managed pig herds. Respiratory disorders and other problems related to inhaling gases, endotoxins, dust, and unpleasant odours are of concern.

In a Saskatchewan study, after three hours of work in a pig barn a large number of veterinary students reported flu-like symptoms. To further investigate this, the students were presented with a questionnaire modeled after the standard questionnaire used for evaluating organic dust exposure. General and/or respiratory symptoms were reported by 72.5%. General symptoms, such as eye irritation, headache, and tiredness were experienced by 42.2%. Cough, nasal and throat irritation, and sinus trouble were the most prevalent respiratory symptoms and were reported by 91% of the students. Symptoms mostly developed the same day and disappeared within three days after exposure. Wearing a mask during the practicum had no significant effect on the symptoms. Students with pre-existing allergies were more likely to develop respiratory symptoms than non-allergic students. It would not be unreasonable to conclude that, with much longer exposures to lower concentrations of barn air components, people downwind of intensive hog barns would experience similar symptoms.

Intensification of pig farming methods has led to greatly increased animal density in pig buildings where several air pollutants may be concentrated. Results of epidemiological studies indicate that this indoor pollution in swine confinement buildings represents a real human and animal health hazard.

The Agriculture Canada Research Branch has reported that ammonia may affect human and animal health. It also noted that political awareness of the odour problem is now growing and that some countries have already established regulations to control odour emissions.

Physiological effects of swine dust on exposed study volunteers included local airway effects and systemic effects, with components of both gram positive and gram negative bacteria. Endotoxin exposure appeared to account for some, but not necessarily all, of the symptomatic and physiologic responses. An array of mediators of inflammation is produced in response to dust components.

Pigs are close to humans in a number of physiological processes. In a behavioural study, two groups of four pigs were continuously observed for 14 days in concentrations of ammonia (0, 10, 20, and 40 ppm) that are frequently recorded in piggeries. An octagonally shaped, eight-compartment preference chamber was built to house the pigs. Each compartment supplied the pigs with ample food, water, and bedding material but differed in the level of atmospheric contamination. Adjacent compartments were separated by plastic curtains, allowing the pigs free access to the neighbouring compartments while reducing cross-contamination. The position of the contamination was changed weekly to eliminate positional preferences. The pigs spent a significantly greater proportion of their time in the unpolluted compartments (53.4%) than in the 10 ppm (26.9%), 20 ppm (7.1%), or 40 ppm (5.1%) compartments. Higher concentrations of ammonia were visited less often and once there, the pigs stayed for a comparatively shorter time (approximately 35 minutes). As the aversion was not immediate, it is suggested that aversion was not due to the odour of ammonia initially experienced on entry.

Instead the aversion may be due to a sense of malaise that may develop while a pig is in a polluted atmosphere. The pigs chose to rest, sit, feed, and forage more in the unpolluted atmosphere. Overall, more feeding behaviour was observed in the fresh air and more food was consumed in these compartments of the chamber.

Multiple Chemical Sensitivity and Hog Barn Odour

An emerging issue in environmental health is the phenomenon of multiple chemical sensitivity (MCS). Multiple chemical sensitivity is a controversial disorder characterized by multi-organ symptoms in response to low-level chemical exposures that are considered safe for the general population. The onset of MCS is often attributed to prior repeated exposures in the home and/or the workplace, and once initiated extremely low levels of many chemicals trigger symptoms.

No single case definition exists for MCS due to several issues that call into question its validity as a distinct illness induced by prior chemical exposure. Hypotheses regarding the etiological basis for MCS range from direct toxicological effects of chemicals to the notion that MCS is purely a psychological belief system. One leading hypothesis suggests that MCS represents a neural sensitization phenomenon, wherein susceptible individuals demonstrate extreme sensitivity to chemicals and odour intolerance due to central nervous system sensitization processes. The recent development of an animal model for MCS provides support for the sensitization hypothesis.

In a recent Belgian study, it was concluded that experimental subjects can acquire somatic symptoms and altered respiratory behaviour in response to harmless but odourous chemical substances (ammonia and butyric acid), if these odours have been associated with a physiological challenge that originally had caused these symptoms. The conditioned symptoms can subsequently be reduced in an extinction procedure.

In the human body, the nervous system may be the part most sensitive to environmental toxicant exposures. A large body of animal research in neurotoxicity indicates that low levels of many environmental chemicals can cause acute and chronic changes in both behaviour and the electrical activity of the central nervous system. Neurogenic switching may be the mechanism that involves multiple organ systems in the situation where a stimulus at one site can lead to inflammation at a distant site. Neurogenic inflammation occurs when a chemical combines with the chemical irritant receptors on sensory nerves. Both the mediators and regulators of inflammation may be released from the site of inflammation and affect distant sites. The role of neurogenic inflammation in a number of inflammatory conditions is currently under investigation. There is strong evidence that neurogenic inflammation is operative in asthma and rhinitis.

Scientific Detection and Measurement of Odours

"Olfactometry" is often used to measure the concentration of odour in air through the use of a serial diluter, or an olfactometer, to present odourous air with odourless air dilutions to a panel of people, often in a specially prepared laboratory. Odour concentration (OC) is defined as the number of dilutions at which 50% of the panel members can just detect an odour. The panelists do not judge the odour but only determine whether they can detect it. The result is expressed as Odour Units (OU per cubic metre).

Odour intensity and odour offensiveness are further odour parameters that are measurable, but are considered more subjective. Odour intensity based on ranking produces a relationship between OC and sensation and is usually described by a power of logarithmic relationship. Odour offensiveness is a ranking of odour acceptability, ranging from extremely pleasant to extremely offensive.

The average concentration of undiluted pig slurry and chicken slurry odour was calculated as 994,000 OU per cubic meter and 67,000 OU per cubic meter, respectively. That is, the average pig slurry odour was 14.8 times more offensive than the chicken slurry.

Odour detection and assessment techniques are costly, time-consuming, and subject to error, and result in delays between sampling and measurement. It is rarely feasible to analyze a sufficient number of samples to map an odour plume over time.

To overcome these problems, several studies have attempted to identify individual volatile compounds in livestock slurries whose concentrations could be correlated with odour concentration. Sulphide content correlated well with odour offensiveness in many instances. Volatile fatty acids, phenols, and indoles were not suitable markers, as correlation between the concentration of these compounds and people's perception of odour were low. Ammonia concentration in air has also been shown to relate to odour concentration, but the relationship is not constant for all farm odours, and odour is still detectable at zero ammonia concentration.

Odourous compounds have also been analyzed by gas chromatography mass spectrometry (GS-MS) and compared with odour concentration as measured by olfactometry. The major odourous compounds were identified as belonging to the sulphide, volatile fatty acid, phenolic, and indolic chemical groups. When four measurement systems—a photo-ionization detector (PID), an Electronic Nose, Olfactometry, and Gas Chromatography—were compared, both the PID and the Electronic Nose instruments were less sensitive than olfactometry. GS-MS was used to demonstrate the differences in the odour chemical composition of pig and chicken slurries. The results showed that some of the major odour compounds are chemically unstable and so it would be helpful to have rapid, portable devices for odour measurement.

Efforts to base odour policy on sound, scientific odour measurement techniques have resulted in major developments in olfactometry and its acceptance as a legitimate environmental assessment procedure. Policies in Australia and North America have tended to be based on the simple avoidance of nuisance, while in northern Europe the quantitative approach to odour policy has been more successful, with workable Europe-wide standards being developed.

Regulations Pertaining To Hog Barn Odours

Odour is regulated as a nuisance and defined as interference with the normal use and enjoyment of property, in every state in the United States. Several states have adopted specific regulations for odour intensity at the property lines as measured using a dilution-to-odour threshold device in most cases. Several states, including Texas, require a construction permit from the Air Pollution Control Agency prior to building a feedlot. Minnesota instituted environmental regulations, including emission controls, more than 20 years ago.

Odours are not regulated by the Clean Air Act in the United States because they are generally regarded as non-toxic. In addition, non-federal legislation for controlling odours is imprecise or lacking in many states. For example, North Carolina specifies that a person shall not cause, allow, or permit any plant to be operated without employing suitable measures for the control of odourous emissions, including wet scrubbers, incinerators, or such other devices as approved by the Commission. This regulation is subjective because it gives no provision for either emission standards or ambient air standards. Under this regulation, it appears that, as long as a plant has suitable control devices, it is lawful for them to emit offensive odours. In addition, it is unclear what type of operation is to be considered a plant.

In contrast, Connecticut's laws on odour emissions set specific standards. Its acceptance limits for some of the volatile compounds associated with fresh and decomposing swine wastes are:

acetic acid - 1.0 ppm
trimethylamine - 0.00021 ppm
ammonia - 46.8 ppm
butyric acid - 0.001 ppm
carbon disulphide - 0.21 ppm
dimethyl sulfide - 0.001 ppm
ethyl mercaptan - 0.001 ppm
hydrogen sulfide gas - 0.00047 ppm
methyl mercaptan - 0.0021 ppm
monmethylamine - 0.021 ppm

In the United States, people exposed to high levels of odour from agricultural sources generally have used nuisance laws to protect their rights. However, there are many caveats in nuisance laws that consider which party was there first, the character of the neighbourhood, reasonableness of the use of the land, and nature and degree of interference. In addition, most states have "Right to Farm" statutes that supersede nuisance laws in some circumstances.

Strong support against nuisance suits involving agriculture is not specific to the United States but is found in the laws of many countries. Suits against agricultural activities based on odour nuisance are harder to prove than those based on water pollution. In addition, nuisance claims fall under state laws, while suits on water pollution are most frequently filed in U.S. federal courts.

In the Netherlands, regulations are based on accurate records of manure production and bookkeeping, and violations are considered a criminal offense. Intensive animal raising in the limited land area in Japan resulted in a large accumulation of animal wastes that have been causing serious pollution problems. Animal farms are now bound by strict regulations to control environmental pollution, especially water pollution and offensive odour evolution.

In Saskatchewan, the Agricultural Operations Act establishes the AgriOperations Review Board. The Board deals with agricultural nuisance issues, including odour complaints if a complaint cannot be resolved locally. No court action can be initiated by a complainant until 90 days after the application has been filed with the Board. If the complaint cannot be resolved, the Board holds a hearing and issues a decision that may dismiss the complaint or recommend the operator cease or modify the practice causing the problem. If either party refuses to accept the decision of the Board the matter can then proceed to court but the court must give primary consideration to the Board's decision.

Odours in Manitoba are regulated under the Farm Practices Protection Act. Complaints are directed to the Farm Practices Protection Board. The Manitoba legislation is very similar to that in Saskatchewan, with the addition that an order made by the Board may be filed in the court and enforced as if it were a judgment of the court. The Board may also, under the direction of the minister, study any matter related to farm practices and report its findings and recommendations to the minister.

The experience so far with this complaint mechanism is varied. One operator in Manitoba's Interlake region was recently ordered for the second time to cover a hog-manure pit to reduce odours. The first Board order was issued in 1996, ignored by the operator and not pursued by the Board. The Board is now threatening, approximately four years later, to use its full powers under the Act.

Citizens affected by intensive hog barns are not satisfied that their interests are being protected by this kind of implementation of the law. The Manitoba Board has ordered six farmers to cover manure storage structures since 1994, a level of enforcement not at all indicative of the level of concern from people forced to live within close proximity of intensive hog barns in the province. By way of comparison the Ontario Farm Practices Protection Board received 600 to 700 noise, dust, and odour complaints against farmers in 1997. Most were resolved with help from agriculture and environment ministry employees. Complaints rarely go to the full committee stage.

Methods of Odour Control

Manure handling technology

Waste management practices can reduce odour production and gas emission via frequent waste removal from the buildings and by preventing anaerobic conditions from developing. Separating the solid and liquid fractions using mechanical separators may ease slurry handling and storage problems.

The FAN Engineering USA, Inc. Slurry Separator produces storable solids that can be composted and which have little smell when applied to the land. The liquids produced contain up to 80% of the plant nutrient value of the original slurry. They can be stored with minimal settling and crusting difficulties and applied to fields at a lower energy input with a lower risk of smothering the crop.

Continuous aeration of liquid swine manure reduces odour production. Indeed, aerobic treatment has been found to be the most effective method to date for deodourizing pig slurry as long as aeration equipment is big enough to prevent odours and functions properly so that anaerobic conditions do not develop.

Although aerobic systems eliminate odours, they have not generally been used in swine odour management. Naturally aerated lagoons or oxidation ponds require large areas. Mechanically aerated lagoons and oxidation ditches have high energy requirements and are therefore considered too expensive to operate.

The Iowa General Assembly in 1996 and 1997 appropriated funds to Iowa State University for support of on-farm demonstrations of artificial cover, aeration, pit additives, anaerobic digester, composting, solids separation, tree-planting, and soil injection as odour control technologies. Agricultural extension agents monitored the odour reduction at each site using olfactometry, particle counters, and citizen odour panels. The results were presented in a video and a series of fact sheets on each odour reduction technology. Many of these same techniques have been successful in reducing swine slurry odours on commercial farms in Saskatchewan.

Barn and herd management practices

The first essential for odour control from livestock buildings is to maintain a high standard of hygiene and cleanliness. The following practices are recommended:

- thorough removal of manure/slurry on a frequent basis (at least every 7 days);
- animals kept in clean and healthy condition;
- buildings regularly and thoroughly cleaned; smooth interior surfaces help;
- bedding materials kept dry and free of moulds and dust; slatted floors stay drier than solid floors;
- appropriate disinfection after each batch of stock;
- proper ventilation to provide a stable distribution pattern of clean air under a wide variety of external weather conditions;

- thoroughly clean and maintain ventilators between batches of stock;
- adequate humidity and temperature control;
- minimize dust and remove regularly; and
- maintain or replace drinking systems to avoid overflow and spillage.

Housing type and manure removal system can have a dramatic effect on ammonia emissions. Emissions were greatest from partly slatted floor systems (21.7 kg / 500 kg live weight), similar from the Danish system or fully slatted floor systems (11.7-12.0 kg / 500 kg live weight), and dramatically reduced in the more traditional bedding systems (1.7 kg /500 kg live weight).

Aerobic manure handling technology

Municipalities and industries have used aeration for years to stabilize waste solids, as well as to control odours. The technology has also been demonstrated to dramatically reduce odour emissions from livestock operations. Aeration has not been widely used in agriculture, however, because of the added utility costs.

A variety of devices can be used to force air into the liquid in the lagoon or storage structure. Ideally, for complete waste stabilization enough air has to be added to equal two times the daily biological oxygen demand (BOD). Less air may be needed just to control odour.

In aerobic treatment systems the products are carbon dioxide, water, sulphates, and nitrates rather than methane, hydrogen sulphide, ammonia, and volatile acids. The products of properly designed and operated aerobic systems are not odourous.

In Iowa studies, where just enough air was added to control odours, the average annual cost of utilities was estimated to be $3 per pig capacity. Floating aerators range in price from US$3,000 to US$6,000 and more than one device is needed for large pits and lagoons. In a large sow facility the per-head cost for the complete system and utilities ranged from $4 to more than $6 per sow annually.

In Japan, animal wastewater, after solids separation, is either treated by the activated sludge process to obtain clean water or by a simplified aeration method to produce liquid fertilizer.

High rate algal oxidation systems have been used to treat piggery waste in Australia, China, and the United Kingdom. High rate algal ponds or reactors are efficient treatment systems that minimize the effects of wastewater pollution by reducing organic matter and inorganic nutrient content. The process also generates heat.

Pig slurry from a 1,200-animal commercial piggery was treated by a relatively small, semi-automatic plant to a level of organic pollution concentration that satisfied the Portuguese regulations for discharge into a surface water body. Over 95% removal of BOD was achieved through intermittent use of the aerator. Aerobic slurry treatment cost US$2.50 per pig produced. A treatment with solids separation followed by 3-5 days aerobic treatment cost between US$2.75 and US$7.50 per pig produced. The intermittent aeration strategy and reduced energy costs as a consequence explains the difference in costs.

Manure slurry barrier systems

The most effective measures for reducing emissions from outdoor slurry stores are covers such as tented roofs, corrugated sheets, floating plastic, and plastic foam. The emission-reducing effect of the various covers depends on the season. It is important to minimize air movement over the surface of the slurry. If done carefully it is possible to achieve emission reductions of 70-to-99% with different covers.

Covers are required in the Netherlands where all slurry storage is in above ground structures. New facilities in Quebec are all above ground storage and covered. Even some rural municipalities in Manitoba have required above ground covered storage structures.

One study by Iowa State University measured a reduction in odour at 50-to-100 feet from the manure pit of approximately 70 % when a synthetic cover was installed. The cost of synthetic covers includes the expense of installing them. Synthetic covers, unlike straw covers, should last for several years and therefore do not incur an annual replacement cost.

In Denmark, smell and vapour are controlled with clay-fired balls about 1 to 2 centimeters in diameter, which are blown on top of concrete storage tanks to a depth of about 20 centimeters (8 inches). In a Danish research study, wood, PVC foil, and Leca (air-filled pebbles of burned montmorillite clay) were compared as covers to reduce ammonia losses from pig slurry storage structures. All materials were very effective. A German product, Pegulit, which consists of self-dispersing granules or powder results in over 95% reductions in odour, ammonia, and hydrogen sulphide emissions, according to laboratory tests. This product is not yet available in North America.

Biocovers are fibrous biological materials such as straw or chopped cornstalks placed (typically blown) on top of liquid storage units to provide a physical aerobic barrier between the liquid manure surface and the air. A variety of materials have been tested, including wheat, oats, and barley straw, hay, chopped cornstalks, hay with oil on it, and barley hulls via the feed ration. Most of the biocovers have worked quite well. In the Iowa State University evaluation, odour panelists judged the odours to be significantly reduced at every distance out to 200 feet. Odour reductions of 50-to-60% were reported.

The success of biocovers depends on season-long flotation and continuous 100% coverage of the storage structure. Biocovers provide an aerobic zone within the material, with a high surface area for filtering and aerobic degradation of odours and other gases emitted from the slurry. Getting an adequate depth of cover is important to accomplishing both of these criteria. Biocovers must be at least 8 inches deep. They are not useful for anaerobic lagoons, which are much larger, have more surface area to be covered, and are open to strong winds that readily redistribute the cover.

Biocover costs include both the materials and the cost of applying them. Unlike synthetic covers, biocovers require annual recurring costs. In Iowa, based on requests for reimbursement for its odour control project, biocovers cost about US$0.10 per square foot of pit surface each time the cover is applied. However, the lifetime of such floating covers is limited and their efficacy depends greatly on their upkeep and replacement. New covers must be applied approximately once each year according to the Iowa State University reports but Purdue University reports they only last 2-3 months.

Odour mitigation via chemistry

A variety of products for reducing odour in manure have been evaluated, but overall the results have been disappointing. A number of different pit additives are available on the market. They include microbes, microbial enhancers, microbial inhibitors, enzymes, deodourants and perfumes, pH adjusters, aeration chemicals, and plant products. Management requirements can vary widely from one product to another. Some products must be applied several times a day, while others need to be applied only once or twice a year.

There are six categories of odour control agents:

- *Masking agents* are mixtures of aromatic oils designed to cover up the manure odour with a more desirable one;
- *Counteractants* are mixtures of aromatic oils that cancel or neutralize the manure odour so that the intensity of the mixture is less than that of the constituents;
- *Digestive deodourants* contain bacteria or enzymes that eliminate odours through biochemical digestive processes;
- *Adsorbents* are products with a large surface area that may be used to adsorb the odours before they are released to the environment;
- *Feed additives* are compounds added to feeds to improve animal performance and reduce odours; and
- *Chemical deodourants* are strong oxidizing agents or germicides that alter or eliminate bacterial action responsible for odour production or chemically oxidize odour compounds.

When 12 odour abatement systems were assessed in a 1992 study, only seven of them were judged to be effective enough to assess how much it would cost to use them. Chemical treatments were found to be prohibitively expensive. Biological treatments and chimneys, although much cheaper, still carried a large overhead per animal.

Several researchers have investigated the use of De-Odorase as a dietary additive to reduce odour from pig slurry. De-Odorase is a commercial powder preparation based on extract of the plant Yucca shidigera. According to the manufacturers, De-Odorase contains selected glycocomponents from this plant that are said to bind ammonia and other noxious gases which would otherwise be released from slurry. The results have been quite variable.

Iowa State University researchers tested several pit additives in the laboratory and found that many did suppress odour production to some extent. However, the results with Shac pit additive, Septisol, and Kane MPC were extremely variable. Pit additive costs include materials and any equipment needed to apply them.

Chemical amendments, such as superphosphate fertilizer, gypsum, sulfuric acid, and lime, have been used to reduce ammonia losses from animal manures with varied results. There are significant reductions in the volatilization of ammonia from animal manures treated with sphagnum peat moss. Acidic treatments, including peat moss, reduced ammonia volatilization from hog slurry by at least 74.6%.

Methane production and capture systems

Anaerobic digestion has been used by municipalities, industries, and some intensive livestock operations to successfully stabilize waste solids, generate methane, and control odours. Methane has a range of possible uses as an energy source, but it has primarily been used by direct burning for heat or as fuel for internal combustion engines. Research studies indicate that several variables influence biogas generation, including pH, volatile acid concentration, temperature, nutrient availability, and toxic materials.

In an anaerobic digestion system, a tank holds the manure while anaerobic bacteria break it down, releasing methane, ammonia, hydrogen sulphide, and carbon dioxide. The digester size is based on the retention time and the weight of volatile solids (the ones that are degradable) produced by the animals each day. For efficient waste stabilization, the solids must be held for 10 to 15 days to allow the bacteria to work. For any anaerobic digester, an additional large storage tank must follow the digester to hold the treated liquid until pump-out time, because very little volume reduction occurs in the digester.

Anaerobic digesters are very effective at controlling odours, nearly eliminating them from associated manure storage structures. Odours remain within the sealed digester during biodegradation. When the biologically stabilized liquid and solids are transferred to the storage pit they produce very little odour.

Agricultural use of anaerobic digestion has been limited by high construction costs and high management requirements for keeping the digester operating properly and safely. However, small hog producers in Manitoba in the 1970s successfully used the technology and generated enough methane gas energy to heat not only their pig barns but also their homes.

In Japan, anaerobic digestion is widely used for animal slurries and biogas is generated and used as an energy source. Slurry spreading is restricted to only a few areas in Japan by regulation. The anaerobic lagoon is actually a type of anaerobic digester. Relatively little research has been conducted on the performance of anaerobic lagoons functioning as anaerobic digesters.

During the summer season in North Carolina, biogas production varied considerably from point to point and over time at a given point on the lagoon surface. Attempts to quantify biogas production and quality using large floating covers found mean biogas production rates for two anaerobic lagoons, one swine and one poultry, ranged from 0.13 to 0.16 cubic metres per day per square meter of covered surface area. Biogas quality (62 to 65% methane) was found to be comparable to that produced in conventional digesters with livestock manures.

Composting systems

Composting as a waste stabilization process for municipal solid waste has grown in popularity over the last 10 years and with that significant technological advances have also been made. As an aerobic process, it has been used for years to control odours, including those from livestock operations. This aerobic, thermophilic process produces a material with several advantages with respect to handling by reducing volume, odours, fly attraction and breeding, and weed seed viability. The heat generated during composting may also destroy pathogens.

Composting systems typically use mechanical devices to provide oxygen to the compost pile, keeping it aerobic. Fans can provide forced air or the windrows can be mixed and turned periodically by specially made turners or front-end loaders.

A variety of research projects have demonstrated that well-managed composting is essentially odour free. However, the major problem in applying this technology to manure slurries is the very high water content of the waste, which requires significant de-watering or the addition of sufficient adsorbent organic materials to absorb the water.

Composting costs can vary considerably, depending on the system and what kind of composting base surface is required. High local precipitation levels may require covering the composting pad at significant expense. Mechanical turners being used in municipal systems can be costly. Tractor turners and front-end loaders provide less expensive but less efficient means of windrow turnover. Closed reactor systems in which the compost is constantly mixed, are expensive and inappropriate for intensive livestock systems as currently constructed.

If a concrete pad is required to protect ground water this also can be expensive. A concrete pad has the added advantage that it provides a firm surface with adequate drainage, allowing the piles to be turned in any weather. In large systems, a leachate/runoff control system may also be required.

On-farm trials in North Carolina successfully demonstrated composting hog manure with peanut shells. Using an ordinary farm manure spreader, Evan Jones, a North Carolina State researcher, mixed waste peanut shells with concentrated pig slurry at a one-to-two ratio of shells to manure. Approximately one tonne of the mixture was piled on a concrete slab. After two days of fermentation, Jones reported little or no odour. In a few days the temperature at the centre of the pile was 65.6 to 71.1 degrees C (150 to 160 degrees F). The piles were turned twice a week with a skid-loader, and no additional moisture was needed. After five weeks, tests indicated the absence of pathogens. The finished compost was a good medium for the growth of bedding plants.

Researchers in the Fraser Valley in British Columbia have evaluated an Eco-Barn system that incorporates composting of a sawdust bedding/manure mixture in a 600-hog grower/finisher operation. The Eco-Barn has proven to be a commercially viable alternative to the conventional feeder barns that use a liquid waste disposal system. The compost is of high quality and supplies excellent markets in organic vegetable production, the greenhouse industry, garden centres, and golf courses. No assessment of odours was provided for the aerated composting process. However, studies have indicated reductions in ammonia emissions with different bedding materials. The Purelean in-barn composting system has been successfully used in Alberta. Compost is the main product from animal wastes, solid or liquid, in Japan.

Dietary management

Another possible alternative is to reduce odour at source by reducing the concentration of odourous or odour-producing compounds excreted in the urine and faeces. Proteins in the pig diet represent one major source of some of the odourous compounds. Better use of dietary crude protein would reduce excretion of surplus protein and so reduce the activity of swine lagoon bacteria, the source of the noxious chemicals. Reducing dietary nitrogen and providing essential amino acids in an ideal protein ratio also reduces the concentration of odourants produced by bacterial action in the resultant slurries.

Ammonia is formed by bacterial breakdown of urea and protein components in the faeces. A lower content of degradable proteins in the faeces can therefore lead to a reduction in ammonia formation. Different feeding regimes affect the nitrogen content of the feed and in the slurry of fattening pigs. By multi-phase feeding, the proportion of protein in the feed can be reduced without any performance penalties. At the same time the nitrogen content of the slurry decreases. With three-phase feeding and the addition of amino acids, nitrogen excretion can be reduced by more than 30% while nitrogen utilization is maintained. However, the synthetic amino acids are expensive.

The addition to the feed of certain enzymes that improve the utilization of proteins will also reduce the level of nitrogen excreted in hog slurry. The supply of protein-poor feed and multi-phase feeding has been demonstrated to lower nitrogen and ammonia emissions in growing pigs.

Dietary manipulation has been demonstrated to decrease nitrogen losses and methane emissions from pig slurry. Changes in the slurry characteristics due to the lower crude protein diet also result in less nitrate leaching and improved utilization of the slurry nitrogen by forage grasses. However, recent studies show that even though ammonia and odours were reduced with a 4% crude protein reduction, pig performance was reduced and carcass fat content increased.

Other measures found to reduce odour production include the use of good quality drinking water low in sulfates and nitrates, diets low in sulphur-containing amino acids, and split-sex feeding to enhance nutrient efficiency and reduce nutrient excretion. The use of proper grinding and/or pelleting has been found to enhance the digestibility of feeds and reduce nitrogen excretion by 20% and 24%. Dutch research has shown that a three-phase feeding program can reduce ammonia emissions 45% and odours 55%. Wet feeding (3:1 water to feed ratio) has been found to reduce odours from 23 to 31% by reducing water and feed spillage. The addition of oils and fats to feed (1% or more) reduced the production of odour-carrying dusts.

Adding fibre sources such as small amounts of soybean hulls or dried sugar beet pulp to low crude protein pig diets has been studied. Addition of cellulosic-type fibre or non-starch polysaccharides can reduce nitrogen excretion and ammonia (up to 68%) and odourous organic compounds. Oligosaccharides can also reduce ammonia excretion by 24%.

Odour absorbers such as calcium bentonite, zeolite, sagebrush, and charcoal can absorb odour-causing compounds. However, pig performance may decrease if fed at odour-reducing levels.

Filter systems

Other odour abatement methods include biofilters or scrubbers. Biofiltration of exhaust air is an aerobic process that breaks volatile organic compounds into carbon dioxide, water, and mineral salts. It works well for low odourant concentrations (under 20 ppm).

The concentration of several odourants found in piggery air was correlated with odour intensity measured by dilution to threshold with the aid of a mobile olfactometer. Odour intensity correlated best with *pcresol*, which has since been used in the Netherlands as an indicator of the efficiency of biological filters in reducing the odour emitted in the ventilation air of hog barns.

Preliminary results of a one-year field study with biofilters and bioscrubbers in two piggeries in Germany indicated reductions in the numbers of particles in exhaust air of 79% to 96% with the biofilter. The bioscrubber system gave only 22% reduction in particles. The biofilter also reduced mesophilic bacteria in exhaust air by 11% and thermotolerant fungi by 71%. The washing water, which is regularly recirculated in both systems, was highly contaminated with varying amounts of air contaminants. The quality of the washing water has a strong influence on the reduction efficiency of both systems.

Specific biofilters for ammonia and hydrogen sulphide have been investigated in Taiwan. The biofilter was packed with co-immobilized bacterial cells, a mixture of Thiobacillus thioparus CH11 for H2S and Nitrosomonas europaea for NH3. The results showed that the removal efficiency remained above 95% regardless of the ratios of gases used. To reach Taiwan's current ambient air standards for hydrogen sulphide and ammonia (0.1 and 1 ppm, respectively) the maximum inlet concentrations should not exceed 58 ppm for hydrogen sulphide and 164 ppm for ammonia with a filter residence time of 72 seconds.

In a further study using compost and dark red kidney bean straw for a biofilter bed, farrowing house odours from a pit fan were reduced by 78% and ammonia was reduced by 50%. In another study, gestation/ farrowing house odours were reduced by 95%, and hydrogen sulphide by 90%. The cost was $US0.22 per pig in this facility.

Manure application systems

Soil injection of liquid sewage sludge has been practised in Manitoba for a number of years in the Brandon, Portage La Prairie, and Winnipeg areas. From personal observation it is a very effective means of reducing anaerobic odours, provided appropriate rates are injected. Public complaints arose in the Portage area when excessive quantities of injected sludge resurfaced and odours could be carried downwind.

Soil injection of manure slurries has also been widely practised in Europe and North America. In the Netherlands and Quebec, regulations require that this technology be used. Personal observations of the practice in the Netherlands in 1995 indicated some problems with over-injection in forage systems. Studies in Europe, Iowa, and Quebec using different evaluation techniques indicate that soil injection can significantly reduce the odour of slurry application to land.

Slurry injection and other technical and organizational measures (time of spreading) have been demonstrated in Europe to reduce ammonia volatilization by up to 90%. Data from Iowa State University demonstration field days measured odour reductions from 60% to 90% with injection as compared to broadcast. The costs of these measures in equipment and time are considerable, however. Iowa demonstration projects carried out in 1997/98 reported that using a slurry tanker to inject manure added about 0.3 cents per gallon, when compared to broadcasting. It was also reported that nutrient savings can offset the cost, more nitrogen being retained in the soil. However, recent research in the Netherlands indicates that, depending on the ammonia/ammonium concentration in the soil and the slurry, ammonia gas emissions may still occur.

Recommendations

Enforceable odour regulations need to be established in the prairie provinces because animal wastes contain high levels of volatile inorganic and organic compounds that can produce strong odours that can impair health in some individuals and destroy the quality of rural life for most neighbours.

Air quality standards should be adopted for ammonia and hydrogen sulphide comparable to those in licenses for industrial and municipal facilities. In addition, the ammonia and methane generated present the greatest risk to terrestrial and aquatic ecosystems. More attention should also be given to other greenhouse gas emissions in addition to methane. Almost nothing is known about the environmental importance of the more than 130 other trace gases that get into the area around pig barns with the exhaust air. Their role should be researched, taking into account recent reports of significant increases in respiratory diseases among people living in areas with a high hog density.

The cost of odour abatement is considered prohibitive by producers and becomes even more so when more than one method is required to control emissions from the whole livestock enterprise. This problem supports the position that the current high water demand slurry system is not sustainable when environmental regulations and enforcement are rigorous.

It is extremely important to apply the *precautionary principle* in matters that may cause adverse effects to human, animal, or plant health, or to the environment. This approach has been adopted by the European Economic Community within the Codex Alimentarius in the field of food safety, health, and consumer protection. The health impacts of offensive odours from an initial scientific evaluation of available information reveals an unacceptable risk, but there is still some lack of information on some specific aspects in Prairie Canada. It is in these circumstances, where an unacceptable risk to health has been identified but further scientific information and research is needed to arrive at a more complete assessment of risk, that the precautionary principle should be applied. Judging what is an acceptable level of risk for society is clearly a political responsibility. Decision-makers faced with an unacceptable risk, scientific uncertainty, and public concerns have a duty to find answers and institute measures to protect the health and well being of citizens under their jurisdiction.

Setback distance guidelines being used by most jurisdictions were derived for barns that implemented maximum factors for building design and management, odour abatement, and land use. Actual distances required to avoid nuisance depend on site-specific wind characteristics—and high winds are a common occurrence in Prairie Canada. Indeed, if no measures are taken to minimize odours at all, then buffer distances of 8 kilometers are probably required on the prairies. This distance should then be reduced by the regulatory bodies as various effective odour control technologies and practices are implemented by the swine facility.

A fully referenced version of this chapter can be emailed to you on request from the author <patonw@brandonu.ca> or from the CCPA-Saskatchewan Office <ccpasask@sasktel.net>.

Chapter 6
The ILO and Depopulation of Rural Agricultural Areas: Implications for Rural Economies in Canada and the U.S.

by Bill Weida

In 1946, anthropologist Walter Goldschmidt used a number of social indicators to demonstrate that rural communities in California surrounded by large farms did not do as well as similar communities in areas where smaller farms were the rule (Goldschmidt, 1946). As the number of large, intensive livestock operations (ILOs) increased, particularly during the late 1980s and the 1990s, a substantial body of literature expanded, tested, and generally confirmed Goldschmidt's work (Buttell, Larson, & Gillespie, 1990; Lobao, 1990; Durrenberger & Thu, 1996; Lyson, Torres, & Welsh, 2001; Welsh & Lyson, 2001). In addition, a number of separate lines of inquiry attempted to explain the unfavourable trends in property values and tax revenues that developed across the agricultural regions of the U.S. and Canada where ILOs were common (Abeles-Allison, 1990; Abeles-Allison & Connor, 1990; Palmquist et al., 1995).

These inquiries all concerned social and economic conditions in "rural areas." However, as time has changed, the composition of rural areas has also changed. Recent effects of these changes occurred in two phases. In the first phase the financial conditions of the 1960s and early 1970s ruined a large number of farmers whose high debt load and high fixed costs precluded their survival during a period of prolonged weakness in crop prices. A secondary result of these failures was the loss of a number of weaker rural communities whose base of support was directly linked to the failed farms that had surrounded them. This loss of rural communities was an ongoing process that weeded out weaker communities while leaving those with alternative bases of support. This, in turn, established the economic environment in which the second phase of change—the ILO expansion period of the late 1980s and 1990s—occurred.

During the second phase of change, those rural agricultural communities that were large enough to have full service economies were able to survive by becoming increasingly separated from the farming and ranching areas and small communities that surrounded them. As Gale (2000) has noted, "[w]hile many view 'rural' and 'agriculture' as virtually synonymous, the ability of the rural economy to shake off severe problems in the agricultural sector is a reminder that agriculture is no longer the primary economic engine of rural [areas]" (pp. 21,22). And this process tends to feed on itself. As those rural towns with full service economies experienced non-agricultural economic growth, they became increasingly able to pull money and business from the surrounding agricultural areas because of the superior level of local services this non-agricultural growth had created.

For this reason, the inquiry proposed here requires a modification of the definition of rural agricultural areas. In the past, rural agricultural areas where actual farming/ranching occurred were viewed in the same way as the rural communities they surrounded. Because this has changed in many rural locations, this chapter differentiates between areas of rural residential concentration—which include rural communities—and areas of rural agricultural activity.

Population Trends in Rural Areas in the United States

While the following figures have been collected for the United States, there is good reason to believe they are also indicative of similar trends in Canada. Figure 1 shows there was a continual shift of population from agricultural to urban areas for the 150 years prior to 1970. Within this phenomenon, the percentage of rural non-farm residents increased steadily from 1930 to 1960 and then fell as rural communities died during the financial crisis I have called Phase 1. However, since the 1970s rural depopulation has slowly occurred in areas of rural agricultural activity—not in areas of rural residential concen-

Figure 1. Rural U.S. Non-farm Population Stability Since 1970

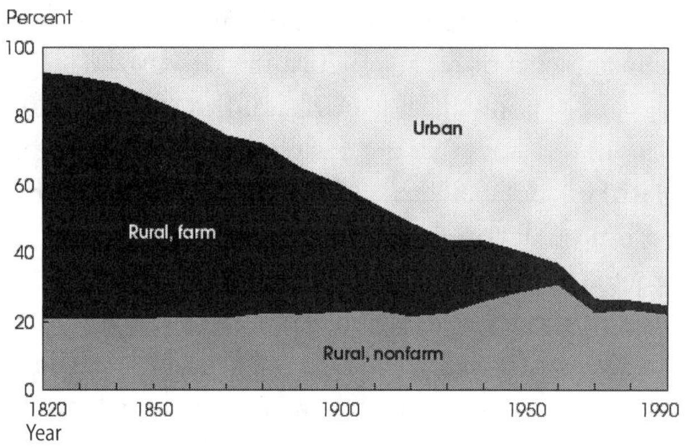

Source: Census of Population data compiled by Woods and Poole Economics, Economic Research Service, USDA, 2000.

tration. Areas of rural residential concentration remained stable and actually grew in the U.S. in the 1980s.

Depopulation in rural agricultural areas is difficult to study because the number of people involved is small even though the land areas involved are large. Depopulation might be accelerated by an ageing rural population which, if it is without heirs (or interested heirs) is motivated to sell and move into rural communities where services are better. However, this factor alone cannot explain why depopulation would occur in rural agricultural regions unless no one else was willing to purchase the land offered for sale by these ageing residents—a condition that should be reflected in generally lower rural land prices. In contrast, land values have continued to rise in rural areas due to recent reductions in borrowing costs and existing tax incentives (Henderson, 2002). Further, demand for rural residences has been high. Recent studies show that people in urban areas want to move to rural communities because of the environment and because they can live in a community where they are known and where they can make a difference. A 1995 Roper survey found that 41% of people polled (up from 35% in 1989) said they would like to live in a small rural town within 10 years (Johnson & Beale, 1998).

Thus, while national attention in the U.S. and Canada has been focused on depopulation in areas of rural agricultural activity, a reverse, coincident trend appears to be occurring in areas of rural residential concentration. The hypothesis of this chapter is that, while depopulation in areas of rural agricultural activity did not initially occur by design, depopulation is now significantly motivated by legal and economic factors that are designed to stifle rural opposition to ILOs. Further, policies enacted by rural residential areas often appear to promote depopulation in the rural agricultural areas that surround them. In combination, these factors degrade the lifestyle of residents and render agricultural land attractive only to owners who do not live on the land, providing a strong rationale for rural agricultural depopulation. As the following sections will demonstrate, given these policies, the resulting outcome (depopulation) was predictable.

The Mechanisms of Depopulation

Large ILOs usually locate in areas of rural agricultural activity, not rural residential concentration. While these operations are a point source of both water and air pollution that falls unevenly across the area surrounding the ILO, air pollution has generally imposed the most significant costs on surrounding residents. Those rural farmers and ranchers closest to the ILO bear most of these costs.

The economic loss suffered by the neighbours of an ILO can be significant. Costs shifted to the residents of the region by an ILO lower the sales and taxable value of neighbouring properties. Palmquist et al., in a 1995 study in North Carolina, found that neighbouring property values were affected by large hog operations based on two factors: the existing hog density in the area and the distance from the facility. The maximum predicted decrease in real estate value of 7.1% occurred for houses within one-half mile of a new facility in a low hog farm density area. Updates of this study in 1997 and 1998 found that home values decreased by $.43 for every additional hog in a five-mile radius of the house. For example, there was a decrease of 4.75% (about $3,000) of the value of residential property within 1/2 mile of a 2,400-head finishing operation where the mean housing price was $60,800 (Palmquist, 1995; Palmquist, Roka, & Vukina, 1997).

A 1996 study by Padgett and Johnson found much larger decreases in home values than those forecast by Palmquist. In Iowa, hog ILOs decreased the value of homes in a half-mile radius of the facilities by 40%, within 1 mile by 30%, 1.5 miles by 20% and 2 miles by 10%. In addition, an Iowa study found that, while some agricultural land values increased due to an increased demand for "spreadable acreage" total assessed property value, including residential, fell in proximity to hog operations (Park, Lee, & Seidl, 1998).

An 18-month study of 75 rural land transactions near Premium Standard's hog operations in Putnam County, Missouri conducted by the Departments of Agricultural Economics and Rural Sociology at the University of Missouri, found an average $58 per acre loss of value within 3.2 kilometres (1.5 miles) of the facilities. These findings were confirmed by a second study at the University of Missouri-Columbia by Mubarak, Johnson, and Miller that found that proximity to a hog ILO does have an impact on property values. Based on the averages of collected data, loss of land values within 3 miles of a hog ILO would be approximately US$2.68 million and the average loss of land value within the 3-mile area was approximately US$112 per acre (Mubarak, Johnson, & Miller, 1999).

A compilation by the Sierra Club of tax adjustments by county assessors in eight states documented that lower property taxes follow these decreases in property value. Local property tax assessments were lowered in Alabama, Illinois, Iowa, Kentucky, Maryland, Michigan, Minnesota, and Missouri by 10-to-30% due to their close proximity to the corporate hog ILOs. Real estate appraisers have also noted the problems associated with property values and large hog operations. In an article in the July, 2001 Appraisal Journal, John Kilpatrick (2001) stated that,

> [w]hile the appraisal profession has only begun to quantify the loss attributable to [ILOs],...diminished marketability, loss of use and enjoyment, and loss of exclusivity can result in a diminishment ranging from 50% to nearly 90% of otherwise unimpaired value. (p. 306)

As a result, diminishment effects continue to be considered when tax valuations are determined around large ILOs. On September 14, 2001, Clark County, Illinois established an assessment abatement for 50 residential homes around the Welsh Farm (a hog ILO) in northeast Clark County. For those homes within a 1/2 mile of the hog production facility, there is a 30% reduction in the property assessment; 25% reduction within 3/4 of a mile; 20% within 1 mile; 15% within 1 1/4 miles; and 10% for 1 1/2 miles (Beasley, 2001).

Resistance and Responses to ILO Losses

As losses of lifestyle and property value resulting from air pollution have been recognized by rural residents, resistance to ILOs has grown in rural agricultural areas. The ILO's response to this resistance is fundamentally determined by the fact that an ILO is structured to view local residents as nuisances instead of assets. ILOs crave isolation, and they are carefully designed to facilitate an isolated existence. They select areas close to good roads and railroads so they can import those things they need to build their facilities. They use/hire very few people and often import those employees who run their facilities. These people usually live far from the ILO site.

To reduce costs, the ILO makes every effort to pay as few taxes as possible. This mandates locating in areas with existing infrastructure or infrastructure the public will finance. This also gives the ILO an incentive to leave an area before the tax base deteriorates and before tax rates increase. The growing separation between rural agricultural areas and rural residential areas can be helpful in this respect. As recent actions in places as diverse as Russell, Manitoba and Dumas, Texas show, a rural community can establish zoning laws or it can use agreements associated with ILO subsidies to keep ILOs away from its own residential areas while still providing tax support for ILOs to locate in rural agricultural areas well removed from the community. ILOs, in turn, are increasingly careful to locate far enough away from any community so it does not feel the effects of the ILO's pollution. If the community believes the ILO will improve its economy, it is likely to support such activities to the detriment of the residents in the agricultural areas around it.

For example, when the Dumas, Texas City Council voted 5-0 to sell all but 30 years of Dumas's water supply to a Seaboard hog slaughtering facility, it carefully arranged to pipe the water to a site 15 miles away from Dumas along the southern border of the county (Storm, 2002). This allowed Moore County, where Dumas is located, to collect taxes on the slaughtering plant while shifting the negative social costs of the plant (housing, educating, and meeting the medical needs of the large Hispanic workforce) south to Amarillo, Texas, where most workers are expected to live. This same agreement will require a large number of hog production facilities to supply the slaughter facility. These are slated for Sherman County, again protecting the area around Dumas.

Because they are intent on finding isolated locations, ILOs are also designed to use out-of-area suppliers. These may be other members of their vertically integrated organization, or they may simply be the lowest cost supplier who ships into the region using the rail or road infrastructure the ILO specified as part of its site requirements. The transportation links the ILO uses to bring its supplies into the region are also used to ship what it produces out of the region. The overall effect is that of a camper in an isolated region who brings what he needs, stays for a while, and departs—leaving behind whatever pollution and environmental damage caused by the stay. Those rural residents who are affected by the pollution created by the ILO, and who are likely to complain loudly as a result, are nuisances to be avoided or removed as expeditiously as possible.

For obvious reasons, activities that lead to depopulation are not accompanied by published statements of intent, but they can often be implied. For example, in 1997 the Canadian Pork Council asked Agriculture and Agri-Food Canada to develop a co-ordinated vision and approach to the environmental challenges faced by the Canadian hog industry. The vision statement forecasts that,

> [e]nvironmental constraints to hog production in Canada will be significantly reduced within the next three years through the joint efforts of government, industry and other

interest groups. (AAFC Hog Management Strategy Development, 1997)

This statement effectively removes residents of rural areas from any role in determining the effect of ILOs on their area and, at the same time, stresses the one factor—reduced environmental constraints—that would make rural agricultural areas undesirable for those residents.

Overt and Covert Depopulation Initiatives

As a result, diminishment effects continue to be considered when tax valuations are determined around large ILOs. On September 14, 2001, Clark County, Illinois established an assessment abatement for 50 residential homes around the Welsh Farm (a hog ILO) in northeast Clark County. For those homes within a 1/2 mile of the hog production facility, there is a 30% reduction in the property assessment; 25% reduction within 3/4 of a mile; 20% within 1 mile; 15% within 1 1/4 miles; and 10% for 1 1/2 miles (Beasley, 2001).The fastest way to remove rural residents and thus depopulate an area is overtly—simply buy out the nearest residents who are most likely to complain. For example, when the Circle Four Facility (planned for 70,000 sows farrow to finish) started in Milford, Utah, residents within a five-mile radius of the facility were bought out. Smaller facilities have employed smaller buyouts. Buyouts are expensive and ILO owners would prefer a cheaper option, but the extensive use of buyouts demonstrates that ILO owners do recognize that the pollution they create is not compatible with residences in the areas in which they locate.

For obvious reasons, activities causing or promoting depopulation of rural areas are unpopular with the residents of those areas. For this reason, the initial method used by ILOs to accomplish rural depopulation has been to do it covertly through existing legislation such as Right-To-Farm laws in the U.S. or similar measures in Canada. ILOs claim to be agricultural operations and as such they seek protection from nuisance lawsuits concerning water and air pollution. In addition, Sullivan, Vasavada, and Smith (2000) found that,

> animal industries tend to move to areas with a lax environmental regulatory structure....[T]he more a state [or province] spends on environmental enforcement, the less likely a given firm will locate in that state [or province]. Differences in level of enforcement among nearby states [or provinces], especially if competitors already operate in the area, may also affect location decisions...Location decisions, while important at the state [and provincial] level, also have an international context, with concerns about large production companies shifting investment outside the US [to areas like Canada]. (pp. 22, 23)

Local control of conditional use permits by counties in most states and Canadian provinces may re-impose other regulations that threaten ILO expansion. For example, Worth County, Iowa resorted to the use of county health regulations to keep ILOs out (Marbery, 2001) and based on the success of this effort, other counties are using the same tactic.

The economics of pollution prevention also tend to favour large ILOs and to drive smaller, conventional operations out of business. This perverse result is important because many ILO costs (feed, antibiotics, interest rates, building supplies, etc.) are fairly uniform. As a result, there is little an ILO can do to avoid or reduce these costs. On the other hand, waste management is generally regulated by county, state, or provincial rules, and national regulations only come into play when significant pollution of federal waterways or some similar activity occurs. Thus, waste management is an area where significant profit-increasing shortcuts can be taken. These shortcuts are likely to degrade the lifestyle of neighbours of the ILO and lead to depopulation.

However, even when the polluting actions of ILOs result in local, state, provincial, or national demands to clean up their operations, depopulation may still occur. Metcalfe (2001) has shown that while increased environmental compliance costs for water quality have no significant influence on large hog operations, they have significant negative effects on smaller operations. This may drive these operations out of business and contribute to rural agricultural depopulation. Acknowledging this, Premium Standard Farms recently stated during an investors' conference that, "[s]tricter environmental and regulatory requirements increase barriers to entry" (Morgan Stanley Investors Conference, 2002, p. 8) in the hog sector. Similarly, a Minnesota study (Jacobson, 1999) found the cost of compliance with certain EPA regulations affects moderate size dairies more adversely than large-size dairies. Large-scale dairies can more easily amortise the extra capital investment costs involved with EPA compliance. This suggests that moderate size dairies that must invest to meet the EPA standards may go out of business if they are unable to expand.

Most environmental standards focus on water pollution, but there is an important difference between water and air pollution when depopulation is considered. Water pollution often takes a significant amount of time to register in wells and other monitoring locations (for example, in eastern Colorado and in the Texas Panhandle it appears to take about 20 years for surface pollution to reach the aquifer). Air pollution, on the other hand, is seldom regulated and it has an immediate effect. Those county-level regulations that have caused ILOs to locate elsewhere directly address the short term pollution concerns that local residents feel would destroy property values and result in depopulation—and those concerns usually involve air pollution.

In the last five years, ILO owners have responded to the growth of county-level regulation by attempting to remove any ability to regulate air and water pollution from the counties and to locate the permitting process in state or provincial governments where political influence could be more easily exerted by ILO owners. In the state of Texas and in the province of Alberta this has created a regulatory structure that relaxed laws for permitting facilities, established lax oversight of existing regulations, and reduced public participation "loopholes." Indeed, in the Texas case not only were the counties rendered powerless, but citizens have effectively lost almost any right of legal redress: Texas laws required a person suing another for a nuisance to pay all court cost for both sides—whether or not they win.

ILOs and the Right of Exclusive Use

Laws that remove the ability of residents to control air pollution on their property attack the right of exclusive use, a fundamental legal principle that states that:

> those who have no claim on property should not gain economic benefit from enjoyment of the property. In other words, the right of use is exclusive to the property owner, and any violation of the right of exclusive use typically carries either payment of compensation to the rightful owner or assessment of a penalty. For example, if "A" trespasses on land owned by "B" then "A" will be guilty of a crime and a possible criminal penalty may be in order, as well as civil damages. Physical impairment, such as odour or flies, in effect is a trespass on property rights and violates the right of exclusion. (Kilpatrick, 2001, p. 303)

Both the legal and economics professions view the right of exclusive use as fundamental to the long-term beneficial use of property. If exclusive use is violated, those who own land cannot be assured of compensation for the use of their property and they will tend to adopt shortsighted land use policies—for example, accepting the pollution of a contract hog operation in return for short-term economic gain. This lowers both the efficiency with which the property is used and the long-term societal benefits gained from use of the property (Snare, 1992; Stigler, 1992).

In the context of this chapter, just as the cost of airborne pollution falls unevenly on the neighbours of the ILO, so does the loss of the right to exclusive use. This, in turn, means that the rural residents around the ILO are more likely to act in a manner that increases their short-term gain at the expense of long-term societal benefits. This is precisely the kind of activity ILO owners desire because it leads to the creation of more ILO sites. Unfortunately, the side-effect of these actions is to hasten the depopulation of rural agricultural areas where ILOs are located as more and more land is rendered uninhabitable due to pollution.

This explanation provides the rationale for certain ILO actions that seem to make little economic sense. For example, why would an ILO, whose main concern is driving down the cost of production, engage in a lengthy and costly legal fight to force itself on a rural area when it would be simpler to just move the site to a more hospitable location? One answer lies in the realization that the legal fight, if successful, will break open the area not only for the ILO owner who is suing, but also for additional ILOs that are likely to follow.

This also provides one plausible explanation for the rapid growth in contract hog operations. On their face, contract hog finishing operations would appear to be at variance with the desire of modern ILOs to be completely vertically integrated (Morgan Stanley Investors Conference, 2002). However, the use of contract finishers allows major vertically integrated ILO owners like Smithfield, Maple Leaf, or Premium Standard to gain entrance to a rural area through a local resident. Once this entrance has been gained, the loss of the right to exclusivity will commence and entrance will be much easier for additional operations.

One could claim that the setback provisions of any ILO permitting regulation, whether they be county or state/provincial based, will prevent the loss of exclusive use that has been described in the previous paragraphs. This is unlikely for a number of reasons. First, setback requirements usually stipulate distances that are considerably less than those that have already been shown to be associated with losses in property and tax values. But even if one could assume that a setback requirement had been properly sized to reduce to zero all problems with airborne pollution, the setback itself establishes an area around an ILO where normal development and normal residences are not permitted unless the owners are willing to waive all rights to exclusive use. In other words, potential residents within a setback radius could only build if they acknowledged they were subject to air pollution and thus waived their rights to exclusive use.

This means that every setback radius becomes a centre of potential depopulation.

The Role of Rural Residential Areas in Locating ILOs in Rural Agricultural Areas

Creation of a moral hazard based on asymmetrical information

A proposed ILO will hide most important information about its planned activities from the rural residents of the region it is entering. Among the residents of the rural region, the rural residential community usually has greater influence than those living in rural agricultural areas—both in terms of numbers (votes) and in terms of the influence of business interests. When an ILO enters a rural region, it strikes a bargain with these rural residents. This implicit contract is usually formed around stated, but not legally enforceable, promises of jobs and economic impact on the region—items that most directly effect the viability of the rural residential area. The ILO promises these things in return for land, water, access, power, and the other factors that are required for the ILO to operate. This contract also implies a certain physical relationship with the region that manifests itself in the presence (or lack) of pollution, traffic, resource consumption, etc., that arise from the operation of the ILO.

The ILO is typically well informed about the legal contract with its vertical organization and the implied contract with the region because it signed the legal contract and it extended the offers on which the regional contract is based. But the residents of the region are privy to very little information about the ILO's explicit contract with its organization. As a result, there is an incentive on the part of the ILO to shift costs between the contracts based on each party's access to information about those costs. The party with the least information about costs is most likely to have those costs shifted in its direction.

Asymmetrical information refers to a situation where one of two individuals in an agreement or contract possesses more information than the other individual about the nature of the bargain. If one individual possesses critical additional information about the contract, this individual can use his proprietary information to gain an advantage in the bargain. Such a contract is likely to increase the profits of the ILO by shifting the operating costs of the ILO to the closest residents around its operation. The certainty of this outcome follows directly from the existence of asymmetrical information about the operation of the ILO and from the motivation of the ILO owners.

Local, county, state, provincial, and national laws and policies on the environment and on zoning are important determinants of the location of ILO facilities (Hennessy & Lawrence, 1999). However, when an ILO enters a region it encounters a set of rules that have generally been structured to control a kind of agricultural production whose inputs and waste by-products are not representative—either in quantity or chemical composition—of an intensive livestock operation. Thus, in addition to being based on asymmetrical information that heavily favours the ILO, the contract with the region is often physically defined around incorrect assumptions.

All these factors create an agreement (contract) between an ILO and the residents of the region based on non-enforceable promises of jobs and economic development, but for which most of the information needed to validly assess the impact of the ILO on the physical, social, and economic environment is withheld from the public and is available only to the owners/operators of the ILO. In such circumstances the permitting agency has created a moral hazard where one party (the ILO) is better informed than the other (the rural residential community) about the characteristics of the transaction. By definition, a moral hazard leads to lower efficiency and to higher costs to the party that is least informed (in this case, a higher cost to the region that hosts the ILO).

As the previous paragraphs have shown, the moral hazard is not uniformly spread across the region. Instead, it is concentrated on those rural agricultural landowners who are closest to the ILO—and who have less political power in the permitting process. This moral hazard manifests itself in loss of the right of exclusive use and it creates an incentive for these property owners to maximize the short-term gains from their property by moving out and selling to other ILO owners.

Rural agricultural property owners are likely to find willing buyers because, having created a moral hazard, the region is now faced with a second economic condition called adverse selection—an incentive has been created for additional producers who also want to shift costs to the residents of the region to migrate to the area (Milgrom & Roberts, 1992).

Since the ILO can only be trusted to act in its own self-interest, the only way out of this situation is for the region to be committed to protecting all of its residents whether they reside on agricultural land or in rural communities. And the only way to accomplish this is to have knowledgeable regulators monitor the ILO. Unfortunately, ILOs use laws based on loose, conventional agricultural standards to avoid pollution controls that would more fully assign the costs of waste to the ILOs. In addition, the factors that make it difficult to get information on proposed ILO operations during the permitting process also complicate attempts to monitor ILOs. This leads to a condition called low separability, "...the feasibility to see who has done the work. With low separability, the principal [in this case, the region] will face either high control costs or intense cheating" (Sauvee, 1998, p. 55, 56).

So far, the history of ILO operations shows that cheating is likely. It is made even more likely by the separation between the rural community where the ILO is approved and the rural agricultural area where the ILO operates. If monitoring fails or is not effectively implemented, the only other option for controlling the behaviour of the ILO is through economic incentives. But a powerful economic incentive structure has already been formalized in the explicit contract between the ILO, its own organization, and its investors. This contract directs the ILO to operate in such a way as to maximise profit, and if it can do this by shifting the costs of its waste to its neighbours in the region, that is how it will operate.

Rural residential motivation for approving ILOs

Rural residential areas—usually the local communities that serve agricultural regions—often recruit and justify the presence of ILOs on economic grounds. However, regional economic development proceeds on the premise that the wages paid and purchases made by a company are transferred to other individuals or companies inside the region. The multiplier effect of these payments further assumes they are again spent within the confines of the region and they do not "leak" into other areas of the state or province. Unfortunately, the economic characteristics that generally define an ILO are fundamentally incompatible with these requirements for rural regional economic development. ILOs are purposely structured so they will not aid regional economic development due to the following economic constraints to their operating behaviour:

Constraints on regional economic development due to employment. As a capital-intensive company, an ILO is designed to minimise the number of workers and hence, minimize the economic impact on the region. A 1998 Colorado State University study found that only three-to-four direct jobs (jobs with the hog producer) are created for every 1,000 sows in an ILO sow farrowing operation (Park, Lee, & Seidl, 1988). Ikerd (1998) calculated that a farrow-to-finish contract hog operation would employ about 4.25 people to generate over $1.3 million in revenue. His figures showed that an independently operated hog farm would employ about 12.6 people to generate the same amount of hog sales. Further, a number of studies have found that, compared with small farms with an equivalent composite production value, a large farm tends to buy a smaller share of consumption and production inputs in nearby small towns (Chism & Levins, 1994; Henderson, Tweeten, & Schreiner, 1989).

Each farm job may add as much as one more job in local communities and another in the state outside the local communities. Similarly, each $1,000 of farm income may add as much as another $1,000 to local communities and another $1,000 to the state outside the local communities (Sporleder, 1997). Either of these figures usually overstates the economic impact of farm jobs on rural counties because the employment multiplier cannot operate at these levels unless all employees both live and work inside the region. Given the ability to commute and the likely presence of air pollution around the ILO, it is likely that many workers will live well outside the region and that the resulting employment multiplier will be considerably less. For example, employees at the Circle Four hog ILO in Utah (now owned by Smithfield) chose long commutes that often took them entirely out of the county to live in areas with less odour and better services.

The size of the employment multiplier further depends on the amount of purchases an ILO makes in the region. Large-scale animal production facilities are more likely to purchase their inputs from a great distance away, bypassing local providers in the process (Lawrence et al., 1994). A 1994 study by the University of Minnesota Extension Service found that the percentage of local farm expenditures made by livestock farms fell sharply as size increased. Farms with a gross income of $100,000 made nearly 95% of their expenditures locally, while farms with gross incomes in excess of $900,000 spent less than 20% locally (Chism & Levins, 1994).

Intensive livestock operations can occasionally benefit local grain and hay sellers, but only when they consume all the grain or hay produced in the county. If the county has to export even one bushel of grain or one bale of hay, all grain or hay in the county will have to be priced at a level that enables them to compete in the larger export market (Hayes, 1998).

Constraints on regional economic development due to taxes. While national tax rates differ from state or provincial rates, taxes are generally levied on the taxable income calculated on national returns. Numerous tax write-offs are often possible because ILOs are sometimes treated as industries and, at other times, treated as farms. For example, Big Sky Farms, a hog producer in Saskatchewan, argues that it is an agricultural enterprise on its permit applications in Rural Municipalities (RMs). But it is also regarded as a small business and receives benefits from the Saskatchewan government based on this designation. If these dual designations lower Big Sky's reported national taxable income, they will also lower the taxes paid in the province of Saskatchewan.

Local taxes in an RM or county are based almost entirely on property taxes. ILOs are usually taxed at rates comparable to other agricultural operations, but they often create additional social, health, and traffic costs the local government must finance. The local government, in turn, must rely on increased property taxes levied across the RM to pay these ILO-induced costs—an increase in taxes that can decrease other economic activity in the region. ILOs sometimes recognise this problem and offer cash payments to offset road and infrastructure costs. Further, remote ILOs often require new power lines because of the energy requirements of the barns and facilities and the construction of these lines can upgrade the services of all power customers along the route.

For example, additional costs associated with hosting an ILO include increased health costs, traffic, accidents, road repairs, and environmental monitoring. One Iowa community estimated that its gravel costs alone increased by about 40% (about $20,000 per year) due to truck traffic to hog ILOs with 45,000 finishing hogs. Annual estimated costs of a 20,000-head feedlot on local roadways were $6,447 per mile due to truck traffic (Duncan, Taylor, Saxowsky, & Koo, 1997). Colorado counties that have experienced increases in livestock operations have also reported increases in the costs of roads, but specific dollar values are not available. In addition, an Iowa study found that while some agricultural land values increased due to an increased demand for "spreadable acreage," total assessed property value, including residential, fell in proximity to hog operations (Park et al., 1998).

Constraints on regional economic development due to adverse local business impacts. In a 2001 study of farming dependent areas, Tweeten and Flora found that if they create environmental problems, newly developed or arrived ILOs might undermine a community's opportunities to expand its economic base. They also found that the vertical co-ordination structure used by large ILOs can cause a loss of resources from farms and rural communities because ILO facilities tend to be so large and because ownership and control may reside in distant metropolitan centres. All else being equal, they found the productivity gains attributed to large ILOs decrease aggregate employment and other economic activities in rural communities.

Rural sociologists Thomas Lyson and Rick Welsh found that agricultural counties without corporate farming laws generally had higher poverty and unemployment rates and lower cash returns to farming. Four hundred and thirty-three agricultural counties—defined as at least 75% of land in farms and 50% of gross receipts for goods and services from farm sales—were studied. Rural community welfare, measured by percentage of families in poverty, percentage unemployed, and percentage of farms in a county realizing cash gains was higher in states with anti-corporate farming laws. States with more restrictive anti-corporate laws also fared better than states with less restrictive laws (Lyson & Welch, 2001).

A study of 1,106 rural communities by Gómez and Zhang (2000) found that large hog farms tend to hinder rural economic growth at the local level. All models in this study indicated an inverse relationship between hog production concentration and retail spending in local communities. Economic growth rates were 55% higher in areas with conventional hog farms as opposed to those with larger hog operations in spite of the fact that economic growth rates had been almost identical in all the studied communities before the advent of larger hog operations in the1990s. Data in the study also showed that communities with heavy hog concentration suffered larger population losses than those with conventional hog operations. According to the authors, the results of this study suggest that, without public policy to protect rural communities, the most probable outcome is the continuing decline of rural communities in the future as the size of agriculture and livestock production units continue to increase.

A second study by Gómez (2002) of 248 towns in hog-producer counties covering the period 1981-1999 demonstrates that smaller hog farms contribute to stronger rural economies and large hog farms are associated with lower economic growth. While there were not significant differences in real retail spending across towns before 1990, if concentration in hog production was 1% lower in town A than in town B after 1990, then annual real retail sales were higher in town A by 0.27%. Such differences, compounded over a fifteen-year period, result in real spending in town A being higher by 4.13% than in town B.

In February 2002, the Iowa Concentrated Animal Feeding Operations Air Quality Study found important emerging issues surrounding the intensification of livestock production that include the socio-economic impacts in rural communities. These issues include declines… in local economic activity and increases in purchases of some animal production inputs from outside the local area, as CAFOs [ILOs] increase in size and number… Studies in Michigan, North Carolina, and Missouri found that the value of real estate close to CAFOs [ILOs] tended to fall. These and other data show that CAFOs [ILOs] are defined by present and potential neighbours as at least a nuisance (Iowa Concentrated Animal Feeding Operations Air Quality Study, 2002).

Conclusion: ILOs, Rural Depopulation and Economic Development

Depopulation is desirable from an ILO's point of view and there are a number of economic reasons why the presence of ILOs is likely to contribute to the depopulation of rural agricultural areas. Meanwhile, the growing separation between rural communities and the agricultural areas that surround them has decreased the likelihood that rural communities will protect their sparsely populated agricultural areas.

Community attempts to recruit ILOs are usually based on fallacious assumptions about the potential of ILOs to replace the economic activity lost through rural agricultural depopulation. Gale (2000) has noted that, as rural residential areas have become more economically independent of rural agricultural areas, "[r]ural communities that can attract service jobs will be the best positioned to grow...the key to survival and growth for rural communities is to develop and attract service-sector businesses" (pp. 21,22). However, this kind of economic development is incompatible with the pollution ILOs create—particularly when this pollution affects the locale where a service-based economy is developing.

Rural communities are becoming aware of this and are increasingly zoning ILOs out of their immediate locale—and into rural agricultural areas whose residents are less capable of defending themselves. Attempts to have rural communities take more responsibility for the future of their surrounding agricultural areas have been complicated by the realization that, as rural residential areas become increasingly tied to service-related activities, the survival of the community has less and less to do with the health of the surrounding agricultural areas. This means, among other things, that recipes for the economic survival of a rural residential area are unlikely to have any positive effect on the depopulation of areas surrounding the community.

Solutions to this problem require a two-pronged approach—the removal of the subsidies and the anti-democratic laws that have led to the expansion of ILOs, and the pursuit of long-run in-migration and economic growth policies that insure the health of the rural communities. Such policies will only succeed if all residents of the rural area realize their fates are inextricably linked in the long run. Short-run policies on the part of either party are likely to create long-run pollution and tax costs that could destroy an entire region.

Recommendations for Countering Rural Depopulation

The problems just discussed are likely to affect both short- and long-term initiatives to restore and develop rural economies. Stauber (2001) has identified four key parts of the efforts to preserve and develop rural economies:

1. Redefine and restructure the rural-serving college and university to increase human capital in sparsely populated and high-poverty rural areas.
2. Create new market demands and linkages to increase regional competitive investments in urban periphery and sparsely popu-

lated areas. Provide incentives for producers, processors, and marketers to enter into new relationships that create profitable supply chains to meet the needs of individual consumers and firms.
3. Develop and use new technology to overcome remoteness to create infrastructure that expands competitive advantage in sparsely populated and high-poverty areas.
4. Encourage immigration to rural communities to increase human capital in sparsely populated and high-poverty areas.

If implemented, these initiatives should generate new technology and new residents for rural regions that, in turn, will provide new sources of economic activity for rural economies. However, none of Stauber's initiatives is compatible with the presence of large ILOs in rural regions. ILOs are major beneficiaries of land-grant college research—research that would be redirected if these colleges were redefined and restructured to concentrate on human capital issues. Thus, ILO owners are likely to oppose any attempts to change the mission of land grant colleges. In addition, ILOs and their vertical organizations often either purchase and shut down local value-added activities like small slaughterhouses or they control these activities through long-term contracts. Both actions create a major impediment to building new supply chains in the region.

Buying time—preserving the local economic base

In addition to the efforts just discussed, each region should attempt to preserve the economy it already has while it attempts to build a new economy for the future. In this respect, no plan for a rural region is likely to succeed unless traditional agricultural operations are preserved. Thus, every rural region has an incentive to preserve traditional methods of agricultural operations—methods that have proven themselves over the long run and that were in place before the problems with industrial-based systems began. How traditional agricultural operations are defined depends on the region of the country and the desires of the residents, but traditional agriculture is important for regional economic development for two reasons: first, traditional agricultural operations provide the economic base from which the region's economic growth springs, and second, these operations are necessary to generate continued public support and to maintain a cohesive community in the region.

Once again, the presence of ILOs in a region is often the catalyst for a chain of events that can make these objectives unobtainable. This happens in the following way: The industrial operation pollutes the air or an aquifer significantly enough that increased regulation is necessary to control the pollution. This results in new laws that are not sensitive to the needs of traditional agricultural producers and, as a result, harm these producers.

For example, in Wyoming a hog ILO north of Wheatland created so many problems that voters in two nearby counties voted in tougher environmental laws governing waste handling and pollution of ground water. This imposed tougher restrictions on local feedlot operators, even though they had not been responsible for the pollution problems. And in Colorado, when a ballot initiative to require covers on hog ILO manure lagoons (among other things) was scheduled for a state-wide vote, opponents of the initiative introduced a second initiative that would have required similar treatment for all other agricultural operations, even though there was no evidence that these operations had caused problems similar to the hog ILOs. The hog ILO lagoon cover initiative passed and the other initiative failed.

In both of these cases, the costs of environmental compliance fell, or would have fallen, hardest on small operators. Large ILOs can spread their costs over more animals and hence suffer a lower per-pound penalty from meeting the new standards. This is a classic regressive tax. It is harder on small operators and it violates the fundamental concept of a pollution tax—that the tax should increase as the amount of pollution increases. For this reason, it is important to maintain local control over pollution control regulations. As a general rule of thumb, as the agency writing the directives becomes further removed from the area where the directives are to be applied, the more likely the regulations are to be insensitive to local desires. However, it is important to note that the regulations would not have been considered in the first place had non-traditional, ILO-type activities not increased pollution problems in the area.

The golden rule of regional economic development

Just as no region can prosper by having its citizens take in each other's laundry (because there is no infusion of outside capital), it is also true that no region can prosper in the long term when one part of the region profits only when another part suffers losses. This method of economic development fails because the profit-loss scenario creates a zero-sum game—any profit earned by some residents that could be invested in the region is nullified by losses to other residents that reduce investment in the region. For regions to prosper, there must be a synergistic effect through the multiplier that is based on the assumption that everyone participates fully in the region's economy through spending and investment. In other words, capital that is brought in from the outside cannot effectively create new wealth and economic growth when one group of residents suffers losses and its ability to participate in this process is cut short.

ILOs and regional investment

The pollution associated with ILOs makes investments in rural regions by other, non-polluting enterprises unlikely. In fact, the presence of ILOs endangers the very rural attributes that might attract investment. The 2001 study of farming-dependent areas by the Council for Agricultural Science and Technology Task Force already cited in this discussion found that if they create environmental problems such as those just discussed, ILOs may undermine a community's opportunities to expand its economic base. They also found that the vertical co-ordination structure used by large ILOs can cause a loss of resources from farms and rural communities and decrease aggregate employment and other economic activities in rural communities (Tweeten & Flora, 2001).

ILOs are also incompatible with in-migration to any rural area. In fact, ILOs stimulate out-migration. The 2000 study of 1,106 rural communities, again cited earlier, found economic growth rates were 55% higher in areas with conventional hog farms as opposed to those with larger hog operations. Communities with heavy hog concentration suffered larger population losses than those with conventional hog operations (Gómez & Zhang, 2000).

ILOs and quality of life issues

Rural regions that follow the economic development model proposed by Stauber must avoid those economic activities that make it impossible for the model to function. Thus, regions must avoid the problems caused by ILOs while making the most of the environmental and social advantages they already have, and the major advantage isolated regions have to offer is their quality of life. While lifestyle is an elusive characteristic, it appears to have three important components—the social environment, the physical environment, and the economic environment. Of these three, the social environment is probably the most important factor in establishing the quality of life.

Many anti-social activities can be controlled through careful zoning, but this only works if the zoning is in place before the decision has to be made. In this respect, it behooves every rural region to carefully review its current zoning regulations. There is a second, similarly important part of social preservation—local control. Rural areas know they are highly subject to arbitrary and intrusive decisions by state or provincial government agencies that respond to outside political pressures, not local concerns, and they should endeavour to establish a firewall against this kind of intrusion. Again, a pre-emptive review of the permitting process followed in the region is the best defence. If zoning regulations and the permitting process demonstrate that a region is serious about preserving its lifestyle, ILOs will look elsewhere.

Avoiding problems that divide communities and stress local budgets is critical because cost of government is a major issue in every rural area. There is simply not enough tax money to run anything other than a small local government. Rural areas should act accordingly and try to minimize those things that drive up the cost of government. The majority of these costs are associated with air and water pollution, social turmoil, excessive use of infrastructure, and depletion of resources—all of which are associated with ILOs and all of which are big ticket items that require rural areas to make large investments of money and people. Companies that are likely to cause these problems should be avoided.

Long-term thinking

Finally, problems and potential solutions for rural areas must be viewed in a long-term manner. There are, unfortunately, no short-term solutions for the economic problems that affect most rural areas. But there are many reasons that short-term fixes should be avoided. Rural areas have extremely limited resources and they cannot afford to repair the problems caused by short-term thinking. Those communities that fall into the short-term trap find that, when they have created a problem they cannot afford to fix—pollution from an ILO, for example—their only recourse is to let in more polluting activities since no other enterprises will consider locating in their area. The only way to avoid this situation is not to get into it in the first place.

To effectively deal with long-term economic and social issues, a rural area must have a plan that is supported by the residents of the region. This plan must incorporate a commitment to both the rural agricultural and residential areas, as well as a long-term vision for the region. This plan must be in place before the offer/threat to the region occurs so the offer/threat can be properly evaluated. All this implies that the future of isolated rural regions is, and ought to be, left in the hands of the residents of those regions. To start this process, the question each region must address is whether it have in place a mechanism to make the decisions it will require to preserve its region's future.

References:

Abeles-Allison, M. (1990). *An analysis of local benefits and costs associated with hog operations in Michigan.* Unpublished Thesis. Department of Agricultural Economics. Michigan State University.

Abeles-Allison, M., & Connor, L. (1990). *An analysis of local benefits and costs of Michigan hog operations experiencing environmental conflicts.* Agricultural Economics Report #536. Department of Agricultural Economics. Michigan State University.

Agriculture and Agri-Foods Canada. (1997). *Launch of the AAFC hog management strategy development approach.* Document received through Freedom Of Information Act, 2001.

Beasley, Lee. (2001). *Cumberland hog facility may affect Clark County homeowners' property values.* Guardian Publishing.

Buttel, F., Larson. O., & Gillespie, G. (1990). *The sociology of agriculture.* Greenwood Press.

Chism, J., & Levins, R. (1994). Farms spending and local selling: How much do they match up? *Minn Agric Econ 676*, 1–4.

Duncan, M., Taylor, R., Saxowsky, D., & Koo, W. (1997). *Economic feasibility of the cattle feeding industry in the Northern Plains and Western Lakes States.* Agricultural Economic Report No. 370. Department of Agricultural Economics. North Dakota State University.

Durrenberger, P., & Thu, K. (1996). The expansion of large scale hog farming in Iowa: The applicability of Goldschmidt's findings fifty years later. *Human Organization 55*(4), 409-415.

Gale, F. (2000). Farming's role in the rural economy. *Agricultural Outlook*, Economic Research Service, USDA.

Goldschmidt, W. (1946). *Small business and the community.* Report of the Smaller War Plants Corporation to the Special Committee to Study Problems of American Small Business. Washington, DC: U.S. Government Printing Office.

Gómez, M. (2002). *Scale of hog farms and economic growth in rural areas: Evidence from the state of Illinois.* Food Industry Management Program. Department of Applied Economics & Management. Cornell University.

Gómez, M., & Zhang, L. (2000). *Impacts of concentration in hog production on economic growth in rural Illinois: An econometric analysis.* Presented at the American Agricultural Economics Association annual meeting in Tampa, Florida.

Hayes, D. (1998). *Iowa's pork industry: Dollars and scents.* Iowa State University.

Henderson, D., Tweeten, L., & Schreiner, D. (1989). Community ties to the farm. *Rural Dev Perspect* 5(3), 31–35.

Henderson, J. (2002). *Will the rural economy rebound with the rest of the nation?* Economic Review. Federal Reserve Bank of Kansas City, Q1.

Hennessy, D., & Lawrence, D. (1999). Contractual relations, control, and quality in the hog sector. *Review of Agricultural Economics, 21*(1).

Ikerd, John E. (1998). Sustainable agriculture: An alternative model for future pork producers. In J. Royer & R. Rogers (Eds.). *The industrialization of agriculture.* Brookfield, VT: Ashgate Press.

Iowa State University and The University of Iowa Study Group. (2002). *Iowa concentrated animal feeding operations air quality study.* Final Report.

Jacobson, L. et al. (1999). *Generic environmental impact statement on animal agriculture.* University of Minnesota, College of Agriculture, Food, and Environmental Sciences. [On-line]. Available: http://www.mnplan.state.mn.us/eqb/scoping.html.

Johnson, K., & Beale, C. (1998). The rural rebound. *The Wilson Quarterly, Spring.*

Kilpatrick, J. (2001). Concentrated animal feeding operations and proximate property values. *The Appraisal Journal.*

Lawrence, J. et al. (1994). *A Profile of the Iowa pork industry, its producers, and implications for the future.* Staff Paper No. 253. Department Of Economics. Iowa State University.

Lobao, L. (1990). *Locality and inequality.* Albany, NY: SUNY-Albany Press.

Lyson, T., Torres, R., & Welsh, R. (2001). Scale of agricultural production, civic engagement and community welfare. *Social Force 80*, 311-327.

Metcalf, M. (2001). U.S. hog production and the influence of state water quality regulation. *Canadian Journal of Agricultural Economics, 49.*

Milgrom, P., & Roberts, J. (1992). *Economics, organization, and management.* Englewood Cliffs, NJ: Prentice Hall.

Morgan Stanley Investors Conference (2002, February 11).

Mubarak, H., Johnson, T., & Miller, K. (1999). *The impacts of animal feeding operations on rural land values.* Report R-99-02. College of Agriculture, Food and Natural Resources. Social Sciences Unit, University of Missouri — Columbia.

Marbery, S. (2001, June 11). Health rules published. *Feedstuffs Magazine.*

Palmquist, R. et al. (1995). *The effects of environmental impacts from swine operations on surrounding residential property values.* Department of Economics. North Carolina State University. Raleigh, North Carolina.

Palmquist, R., Roka, F., & Vukina, T. (1997). Hog operations, environmental effects, and residential property values. *Land Economics, 73*, 114-124.

Park, D., Lee, K-H., & Seidl, A. (1998). *Rural communities and animal feeding operations.* Department of Agricultural and Resource Economics, Colorado State University, Ft. Collins, CO.

Sauvee, L. (1998). Toward an institutional analysis of vertical coordination in agribusiness. In J. Royer & R. Rogers (Eds.), *The industrialization of agriculture.* Brookfield, VT: Ashgate Press.

Snare, F. (1992). The concept of property. *American Philosophical Quarterly, 9.*

Sporleder, T. (1997). *Ohio food income enhancement program.* Agricultural, Environmental, and Development Economics Department. Ohio State University.

Stigler, G. (1992). Law or economics? *Journal of Law and Economics, 35*, 455-469.

Storm, R. (2002, January 23). Dumas ok's sale of water. *Amarillo Globe News*, Amarillo, TX.

Stauber, K. (2001). Why invest in rural America—And how? A critical public policy question for the 21st century. *Economic Review*, Federal Reserve Bank of Kansas City, Second Quarter.

Sullivan, J., Vasavada, U., & Smith, M. (2000). Environmental regulation & location of hog production. *Agricultural Outlook.* Economic Research Service, USDA.

Tweeten, L., & Flora, C. (2001). *Vertical coordination of agriculture in farming-dependent areas.* Council for Agricultural Science and Technology. Task Force

Report No. 137. Department of Agricultural, Environmental, and Development Economics. The Ohio State University and North Central Regional Center for Rural Development. Iowa State University.

Welsh, R., & Lyson, T. (2001). *Anti-corporate farming laws, the Goldschmidt Hypothesis and rural community welfare.* Paper presented at the Rural Sociological Society in Albuquerque, NM.

From Pork to Fork, Green Eggs and Ham

by Brian Storey

You've known for years about green eggs and ham
"The eggs are rotten and the ham decayed," says Sam.
"I will not eat them with a fork
Especially if it's from factory-raised pork!
I hate the smell; how it ruins the air.
You feel like gagging—almost anywhere.
Too much ammonia spread on the land
And hydrogen sulphide drift," says Sam.
"And carbon dioxide and methane emissions into the air
To cause global warming." "Sam, you're making me scared!"
"What about smog agents—nitrogen compounds? Beware
A hundred and fifty agents of disease!
Some are airborne in the breeze.
Don't forget flies, even liver flukes!
Sorry if this line makes you puke!
Enterococci, campylobacter—crytosporidium too.
That resist drug therapy are in the lagoon.
Tapeworm eggs, staphylococcus, salmonella strain
Can cause such sickness, cause such pain."
"But what when a sewage pit springs a leak?"
"Why, we're without a paddle up the falsely labelled NUTRIENT CREEK!!!!"
"Why can they build something that pollutes so bad?
And drives small farmers off their land?
Brings down hog prices, to sell to the U.S.A.—even to Japan?"

"It's because of MEGA incorporation,
And vertical integration
And MEGA-conglomeration, aggregation."
"An aggravation," says Sam,
"An abomination in the nation!

"Damn," says Sam.
"Should we sell our house fast?
The stink is risin' far and foul on a toxic horizon!
Let's save our assets—save our bacon!
We can't just live on GREEN EGGS and HAM!"

Chapter 7
My Story: How I Was Thrown Into the World of Factory Farming—Taiwan Sugar Corporation vs. The County of Forty Mile Residents

by Lisa Bechthold

Almost three years ago, I was living on my farm in the County of Forty Mile in Southern Alberta near the U.S. border. I was not in any way politically active and did not give much thought to environmental issues. In fact, the term "environmentalist" was a negative word and to be an "activist" was even worse! Little did I know, but I was about to engage in the political and environmental battle of a lifetime that would forever change not only my life, but also change the way I viewed the world.

In May of 1999, while at a graduation party at a neighbour's house, one of our other neighbours said to us, "So I guess you'll be moving." Of course we had absolutely no idea what he was talking about. After all, we were living on a third generation farm, my husband had farming in his blood, and we had every intention of retiring in the community of Foremost. We asked him what he was talking about and he began to tell us that the Taiwanese were going to locate a massive hog operation in our area and how we would have to sell out because we would not be able to stand the smell. We went home later that night and never gave it much thought.

In the spring of 2000, as we were busy getting ready to seed, people started poking around trying to buy land, and shortly, the rumour of pigs moving in began to circulate. Soon after, we discovered that Taiwan Sugar Corporation was coming to town and bringing with them approximately 80,000 hogs and of course, the promise of millions of dollars for our dying community, jobs, a market for locals to sell feed grain, and free fertilizer for surrounding farmers. Sounds pretty good, does it not? It also sounded great to many in the area who were concerned our village was dying. Instead, the company brought lies, mistrust, and a split to our community that may never be repaired.

We began to hear about open house meetings being held in our County offices. Of course the neighbours were never officially notified that anything was going on. We began to hear rumors that Taiwan was coming to town. My husband and a few others had begun to attend these come-and-go meetings to try and get some idea of what was being planned. They soon discovered that the information might vary, depending on when you attended and what you wanted to hear.

As a result of lack of information and the men being busy in the fields, my husband said three little words to me. Looking back, I am sure he wishes he had said, "I love you," but instead, he said, "Look into this." So I did. I quickly grew a phone out of my ear, speaking to biologists, agronomists, swine specialists, neighbours of existing operations, and the list goes on. Not one of these people said, "Congratulations, you should be so excited!" Instead, I was told that this was just too big and that I should fight it. So, my husband became a bachelor again as I was launched into the world of learning about pigs, manure, application rates, water usage, health impacts, and economics.

My husband's shop quickly became a gathering place where people came to talk about what was happening and to find out what new information I had uncovered about the impacts of factory farming. We decided that rather than having to keep repeating the information, we would hold a meeting in our home and present some of the information I had been gathering. So we invited families from the area. I put together some packages of information and I made a small presentation in our living room. Little did I know that this would be the first of many to come. It was at this first meeting that Carol, my closest neighbour, asked, "Where do we go from here?" It was then that the decision to fight the proposal was made and we immediately started organizing.

We quickly learned that our local officials were wining and dining Taiwan, giving them free office rental at the County office, and had known about the possibility of Taiwan coming to town for three to four years. They were obviously going to be of no help to us. In fact, they were bending over backward to help Taiwan. The Reeve of our county and the mayor of our Village brought Taiwan to town and the councillors were promoting the proposal. Like in other rural communities, people trusted them, had known them for most of their lives, and had no reason to believe they would bring something harmful to our community.

We realized that rather than doing their homework the councilors would instead take the public relations firm's word as the truth. After all, along with the Alberta government which had gone on a trade mission, the councillors were telling Taiwan that we had lots of land, lots of water, few regulations, and few people.

We asked our County members to hold a public meeting instead of the come-and-go open house that Taiwan was holding. But of course they felt that what Taiwan was doing in the way of informing the public was adequate. One of the reasons that we felt a public meeting, where people could hear the same answers at the same time, should be held was that different people were being told different things. So Carol and I went to one of the open house meetings armed with a tape recorder and began to ask questions. We were told that an above-ground storage tank was no more environmentally friendly than an open-pit lagoon, and other nonsense. Let us just say, that after using some of their comments that were on tape, we were never allowed to use a tape recorder again.

Due to the fact that our own County would not hold a public meeting, we organized one. We rented the Community Hall, mass mailed a "Did You Know" fact sheet with details of the proposal and the meeting, and we brought in a biologist and an Alberta Agriculture soil scientist, who specialized in research on soil fertility, to discuss the pros and cons of using hog manure as a fertilizer. Out of fairness, we also invited Taiwan's engineering/public relations firm to our meeting. We wanted everything to be above board, in contrast to how things were being done on the other side. At this meeting we learned that manure can carry 25 diseases and that it is so rich in phosphorous that it needs a humongous land base for proper application. Of course the applicant interjected that they would use "state-of-the-art technology." We did not think that digging a hole in the ground and filling it with manure was state of the art.

As our County did not have the resources to look at the proposal, they referred it to Alberta Agriculture to do a technical review. The same soil scientist that we had speaking at our public meeting was asked to review the proposal by his peers. Taiwan was proposing to use, with the support of the government and the County, a land base of approximately 12,000 acres. According to the soil scientist, in order for the proposal to be sustainable a land base of about 40,000 acres to 93,000 acres, worst-case scenario, would be needed. Uncapped wells that would be direct pathways for pathogens were also a big concern of the soil scientist. I am sure this will not shock you, but he was quickly removed from the project at the request of the engineering firm as it thought it was being treated unfairly.

We kept educating the public through media releases and letters to the editor that covered different topics each week. We also took out our own ads to advertise the public meetings and our concerns. Because we did not have any experience raising hogs, we decided to go to the experts, people in the county who were actually raising hogs. So we began to visit local Hutterite colonies to find out what their farming practices were when spreading manure. Of those who spoke out, they were concerned about airborne disease and competition. They also said that this operation was just too big and would run them out of business.

We were called fear mongers, the noisy minority. I received hate mail, and it was said that our fight was purely an emotional one. Taiwan's engineering firm kept insisting that the decision would be based on the facts. This is probably the only thing we will ever agree on. We handed in a four-foot high stack of studies and documents citing the negative impacts, including studies from the Harvard Business School and a University of Iowa study on the mental and physical health of people living near large hog operations. Taiwan's side handed in one study written in 1966. All of this time, our County was bending over backward doing everything to accommodate Taiwan while alienating us, treating us like the enemy. At public meetings, we outnumbered the potential land sellers 5:1.

With the help of Bill Weida from the GRACE Factory Farm Project and Scott Dye from The Sierra Club (U.S.), we were successful at both the Municipal Planning Commission and the Sub-Division Appeal Board.

Taiwan's engineering firm still claims to this day that our fight was won through emotion and public pressure, but we know that it took hard work, a strong, organized local group, and that the truth won out in the end.

Was emotion involved? Yes, but it was because we had the facts and were trying to preserve our quality of life for future generations.

Were we against change? No.

Were we against livestock production? No. In fact, most of our core group consisted of multi-generational ranchers and hog producers who have been raising livestock for generations without causing the problems we see today with large operations and without being a nuisance to their neighbours.

Were we against damaging our environment and quality of life? You bet!

My whole world has been changed by this experience. I now work as the only Canadian consultant for the Grace Factory Farm Project, based out of New York. We help communities organize, strategize, and educate themselves. We also provide expert testimony when we can.

In January 2002, the Alberta government took away local control over the ILO approval process and gave it to the Natural Resources Conservation Board. This board sites, approves, reviews, and enforces confined animal feeding operations (CAFOs). As a result, in Alberta, we formed the Society for Environmentally Responsible Livestock Operations (SERLO). I am the vice-president of this society and we review technical information for new proposals, keep an eye out for enforcement orders, act as watchdogs to the board, and promote more environmentally and people-friendly practices. The regulations being promoted by the government are those designed for traditional family farms, ranches, and producers, and they are not designed for the large industrial operations we are being faced with today. These regulations are at best minimal and Albertans deserve more than that. I know that if I did the bare minimum at my job or as a parent, I would be fired, and my children definitely deserve more than the minimum.

Lessons Learned

I would like to conclude with some of the lessons I have learned in the last couple of years:

1. Family farmers ARE environmentalists because they are preserving the land for future generations.
2. I have learned that corporations operate factory farms to use and abuse the land strictly for profit and that they do not care how they treat neighbours or the environment.
3. I have learned that we should learn from the mistakes of other countries like Taiwan, Denmark, and the U.S. to keep from repeating them, but that our government will not listen because it thinks it could not happen here.
4. I have learned that being a good neighbour means people come first—not money.
5. I have learned that you can not believe everything you hear; you have to check it out for yourself. If you can not be bothered, then you have no right to complain later.
6. I have learned that someone telling me I cannot win only makes me fight harder.
7. I have learned that government looks after industry and not the people it is supposed to be representing.
8. Most importantly, I have learned that even though there are people who have sold out to the industry, there are still good people out there willing to do the right thing, even when the personal cost is high.
9. I have learned to hate the phrases "meets and exceeds" and "state of the art technology." Remember, the Titanic was "state of the art" and it sank!

Concluding Thoughts

A short time ago, while speaking to a group of university students, one of them asked me if knowing what I know now, with everything I have gone through and the time that fighting Taiwan took away from my family, would I do it again? YES, without hesitation. I can look at other areas where massive barns are located, and I do not have to guess at what would have happened. I know. I can see firsthand the effect they have on people and the communities in which they are located and I have to ask myself, when did we lose the right to clean water and air? What started out as a "Not in My Back Yard" issue has become a "Not In Anyone's Back Yard" issue.

I no longer let the water run when I brush my teeth; I now recycle; and I make sure that I vote every time. I am slowly getting used to the term environmental activist and am proud to instill in my children that there are times when you can not be worried about voicing your opinion, making people think, or questioning those public officials you are supposed to trust.

My advice to you, if corporate agriculture comes to your town, is to do your homework, and decide for yourself. The following pages include samples of petitions, letters to the editor, and a checklist that may help if you are faced with a factory hog farm.

Call To Action
Opposition Notice to Hog Factory Farms
What Can You Do to Help?

1. SIGN THE BELOW LETTER REQUESTING THAT OUR MUNICIPAL PLANNING COMMISSION, OR ANYONE INVOLVED IN MAKING DECISIONS ON PERMIT APPLICATIONS, TURN DOWN ANY PERMIT APPLICATION REGARDING TAIWAN SUGAR CORPORATION'S PROPOSED HOG BARNS WITHIN THE COUNTY OF FORTY MILE. Include signature, printed name, and address including postal code and phone number.
2. Talk to County Councilors and your MLA to let them know your concerns.
3. Mail this letter to: Box 296 Foremost, AB. T0K 0X0 OR phone 867-2202 (Lisa Bechthold) or 867-2363 (Carol Hougen) OR fax it to 867-2658 (Lisa), 867-2463 (Carol)

Please have them in by July 7, 2000. Thank you.

TO: Municipal Planning Commission

RE: Proposed Hog Factory Farms
Request for rejection of any municipal permit applied for on behalf of the Taiwan Sugar Corporation.

Please accept this as a formal objection to the Taiwan Sugar Corporation's proposed hog barns within the County of Forty Mile.

We are concerned as to the adverse health, environmental, and economic implications of huge factory hog farms, including water and air pollution and associated human health risks, increased animal disease risks, soil degradation from over application of nutrients, and increased vehicle traffic and degradation of County roads. There are not appropriate provincial or municipal guidelines in place to adequately protect our residents, our environment, or our land against these mega hog factories.

We are concerned that county residents will bear the environmental, social, and economic costs and experience very little economic benefit. We are individually concerned because of one, or all, of these effects.

Proposed Hog Barns in Foremost Area Did you know...??

As you may or may not be aware, the County of Forty Mile Council is trying to land the Taiwan Sugar Corporation's huge hog operation. At first, our initial concern was how the odour would affect our daily lives. However, as we gathered more information through Agriculture Specialists, scientific studies, biologists, and people living near large hog operations, we became increasingly concerned with environmental and health risks that would impact the entire County.

- The Alberta Government hopes to increase hog production in the province to approximately 10 million by the year 2005.
- A 7,200 sow(farrrow to finish, approx. 81,000 hogs) operation will produce at least 37,958,400 gallons/year of manure. That is a lot of manure to spread around!!!
- The manure storage of these hogs is in the form of a 400-day lagoon per site.
- Taiwan Sugar Corporation has stated that it will be testing the soil at each lagoon site to see if there is high enough clay base that a lagoon liner will not be needed. So in essence, it may or may not use any liner in these sewage lagoons. Other countries are now being *forced* to use other methods of storing this hog waste due to environmental reasons.
- A spokesperson for TSC was quoted as saying, "Mounting environmental concern and criticism in recent years has made it hard to raise hogs in Taiwan. Canada is such a huge country and we can easily find a place without residents nearby."

- One of the proposed sites is ONLY approximately 4 miles from the Village of Foremost.
- DGH Engineering states in its information package on behalf of TSC that, "should TSC be successful in Alberta, other farms and a small specialized meat processing facility to produce pork for specialty offshore markets may follow the initial venture."
- TSC has stated that it is abiding by the Alberta Code of Practice (COP). Recent research suggests that recommended guidelines for manure management are not adequate because: Recommended manure application rates are too high, especially for phosphorous. Regular soil and water testing on areas receiving the manure ARE NOT recommended.
- The COP, which was drafted by the government, has not had the foresight to include guidelines for Intensive Livestock Operations (ILOs) of anything close to this size.
- Many U.S. states have severely restricted and even closed their doors to mega hog operations due to negative environmental effects and to preserve family farms and small communities.
- North Carolina, where lagoon spills have destroyed farmland and water quality, now have a law in place that only allows new units if they are going to use innovative waste management systems that DO NOT incorporate lagoons.
- Iowa has limited farms to 1,300 hogs due to manure spills. Kansas and Nebraska have banned FACTORY FARMS in favor of smaller family farms.
- The risk of water quality problems increases as the intensity of livestock operations increase.
- There is no such thing as 100% sealed lagoons. A certain amount of waste seeping into the ground is considered acceptable.
- There are a number of SHALLOW SEAMS that seep out of the coulee banks, many of which have been sited to seep into the 40 Mile Dam.
- The presence of pathogens (disease causing organisms) in hog waste applied to land, antibiotic resistance, dust, and heavy metals in lagoon sludge are potential concerns. Nitrates in the groundwater are implicated through association, to cause cer-

tain types of stomach cancer and heart disease in humans, but considered the DIRECT CAUSE of blue baby syndrome in infants.

- The National Institute for Occupational Safety and Health has issued warning for several years to workers in animal confinement operations about job-related asthma.
- A recent study in North Carolina has predictably found that odour from hog operations can negatively impact neighbours.
- Arlene and Dan Calon, who live near a hog operation near Drumheller, state that, "We were hoping that promises and statements made that the 'odour would be minimal' would be true. With each day that has passed by, the odour has become a more intense, gagging, putrid smell."

Effects on soil

- Soil specialists recommend manure is applied on a 4-5 year rotation for continuous cropping and a 6-year rotation for summer fallow.
- The nutrient content of manure does not match the nutrient requirement of the crop.
- Pig manure contains LOWER LEVELS OF NITROGEN and HIGHER LEVELS OF PHOSPHOROUS. If it is applied to meet the nitrogen levels, there will be high and harmful levels of phosphorous. This could also cause decreased crop production.

Conclusion

Much of the land in our community has been passed down through generations. We are stewards of our land in the hopes of passing it on to our children and grandchildren. It is our obligation to not only look after our land, water quality, and the well being of our community but to consider these aspects for our future generations.

It is proven that large intensive hog operations in other countries and other provinces have resulted in negative environmental effects and dramatic changes in rural communities. *We can learn from the experiences of others.*

There are many negative short and long-term effects that an operation of this magnitude will have on our community. These issues need to be addressed *NOW* instead of when it is already too late. Is our community setting itself up to become a glorified landfill? Is the economic benefit worth the effects on our health, water quality, and our land?

Hog Informational Meeting
Tuesday, April 11
7:00 p.m.
Community Hall
<u>Agenda:</u>
Dr. Paul Lewis - Parasitologist
Dr. Ross McKenzie - Research Scientist, Soil Fertility
Health & Environmental Issues
Question Period

Everyone Welcome

County of Forty Mile Residents for Public Health and Environmental Responsibility

Sample of Letter to the Editor

Re: Proposed Taiwan Sugar Corporation hog factory farms in County of Forty Mile.

Taiwan Sugar Corporation is proposing to build a 7,200 sow (farrow to finish) operation within the County of Forty Mile. There will be 5 sites—3 north of Foremost and 2 in the Etzikom area.

We have formed a group within the County which is opposing this operation. We have spent many months doing the necessary research on such a venture. As we read through the massive amount of information, we realized that not only was our County not ready for an operation of this magnitude, but this was also something that was definitely not in the best interest of the people living within. History throughout the world shows that these large hog factories have a negative environmental, health, and social impact on the communities in which they are located. Our concerns include:

1. Negative Environmental Impact.
2. Negative Health Impacts.
3. Odour and all that it entails: That means the potential health hazards, respiratory distress, nausea, dizziness, headaches, flu-like symptoms, quality of life issues, and anything else that naturally goes with this issue.
4. Land Values: In the U.S., land values have greatly decreased near hog operations that are only a fraction of the size we are being faced with. We are very concerned with the fact that our land values will go down as well. People will not want to move into an area that houses hog factories or farm land that has been over saturated with manure.
5. Over application of Manure: DGH Engineering, a promotion firm based out of Manitoba, has stated that we should be able to apply manure to our land year after year on the same piece of land. We have talked to many agriculturists and local pork producers who inform us that once every 3-4 years would be the safe way, and that applying it to our land every year would sim-

ply be "stupid." This would cause problems with crop production, health issues, air quality, and water quality. This is simply not sustainable agriculture.

6. Lack of Regulations: We feel that there are not nearly enough regulations or guidelines in place to make this safe. The Code of Practice, which is only minimal guidelines, is currently under revisement but will not be ready in time.
7. Social Impacts: Management and upper level positions will be filled by the Taiwanese. Most of the other jobs will be "dirty boots" jobs. Jobs within the barns are hazardous to the workers' health. The constant influx of low paid workers will create a higher crime rate and more social problems within our small community.
8. Damage done to County Roads.

We have been circulating a petition throughout the entire County, and to date we have the signatures of over 465 landowners and citizens who are opposed to this project. This number is growing daily. TSC held an Open house on April 12, 2000, which was attended by 125 visitors where only 50% were in support of the project.

We feel that it is the responsibility of our County representatives to listen to the concerns of this many ratepayers.

For further information contact:

Spokespersons for the County of Forty Mile Residents for Public Health and Environmental Responsibility
Lisa Bechthold
(403) 867-2202

Carol Hougen
(403)867-2363

Checklist For Fighting Concentrated Animal Feeding Operations (CAFO'S)

1) **Organize those who are opposed to this CAFO together & give your group a name.** Try to come up with a positive name.

2) **Get the facts.** Look for studies on the negative environmental effects, negative health effects, loss of land values, negative social impacts on communities, cost to county infrastructure, etc. If you base your campaign on factual information you will maintain more credibility. Although emotions have their place in this (after all we are fighting for our quality of life), it is more effective to have proof in hand about the fact that these operations will most definitely have a negative effect on your community in many aspects. Talk to experts (soil specialists, water experts, municipal planners, and microbiologists). Talk to people who live around barns and get them to write letters about how it has negatively affected/impacted their lives. We have numerous studies that we can provide you with BUT studies alone will not win the battle. It is much more difficult for the municipality to approve something if the majority of the community is opposed to it.

3) **Find out what your county bylaws state.** Is the bylaw in place for Intensive Livestock Operations stated as Discretionary use/ Permitted use?

- **Discretionary Use**: one in which even if the applicants have met the necessary requirements as set out in the land use bylaw—they must still convince the decision maker that the proposed development is a good and appropriate use of the lands.
- **Permitted Use**: one in which if the developers meet all of the necessary requirements set out in the land use bylaw they will receive their development permit automatically—as a matter of entitlement or right.

4) **Find out what the appeal process is for your county/municipality** (dates, proper procedures, etc.).

5) **Get a copy of the proposal application.** Review it in detail to find out what they are proposing to do. Do they have: a large enough land base for the spreading of manure? What are the exact land locations of manure spreading lands? Do they have manure-spreading contracts in place? Where are they obtaining their water? Do they have a water license in place? How much water are they proposing to use? Are there any abandoned/uncapped wells on site/on manure spreading lands? Are the minimum distance separation requirements being met? How often are they proposing to put manure on the lands? Are the lands suitable for manure application? Are the lagoons going to be lined with a synthetic liner/a clay based liner?

6) **Organize a public informational meeting** to let community members become aware of the effects of these CAFOs on the communities in which they locate. You may wish to have some experts on hand (Eg. Soil specialist, microbiologist).

7) **Circulate a petition** opposing the CAFO. (We have included a copy of the petition that we used.) Keep the names on the petition confined to those 18 years of age and older and try to collect the names of only those who live within that county/municipality. This will give the petition more credibility. If lack of time is a factor, you may want to put the petition in your local paper. A whole page ad is a great way to get people's attention. We advise running it for at least 2 weeks in case people miss it the first week.

8) **Purchase a large map of your county/municipality. Highlight the lands of those who are opposed to the CAFO in a bright colour.** Highlight the barn sites in a different colour. If the majority of lands being used for manure disposal are located outside of a 5 mile radius from the proposed barns highlight these lands in a different colour (the purpose for this is to prove that it is not as economically feasible or safe to transport the manure such a great distance and also

it will cause a great deal more damage to the county infrastructure). Question how the manure will be transported such a great distance (Eg. Trucks, pipeline, etc.). This map will be a great visual effect as to the amount of opposition to the CAFO.

9) **Start to send out press releases** to inform the public that you are going to fight this and that you will not be going away. (We included a few copies of the press releases that we sent out to give you some ideas.)

10) **Let your County officials know that you will be having your land appraised.** Do this before construction begins. Once the operation is in place you will have the lands re-appraised and the County will be held accountable for the loss of property values. (We have enclosed a letter, which can be sent.) Get neighbours to send it as well. Also, let them know that you will be having your water tested before construction to establish baseline levels for future use.

11) **Send lots of letters.** Letters to the editor, to the county/head office of your district, to local polititians. Get all those who are opposed to the CAFO to write letters. These authorities need hard evidence such as letters. Phone calls can always be ignored. Make sure you keep copies of all the letters sent.

12) **Keep accurate records.** Record the date and time of phone calls, meetings etc. You may have to refer back to them at a later date.

13) **The GRACE website** www.factoryfarm.org. has a lot of information that your group may find useful.

*** Things that will be useful to us:

1 Permit application or proposal.
2 Your bylaws or procedures.
3 Time Frame: what are your meeting dates, hearings, and deadlines in regards to this proposal?
4 Specifics of the proposal: size, location, who, what, etc.

5 Specifics of your area (that would include any information that pertains to your area—water, rivers, streams, slope of the land, any significant environmental areas).

These are just a few ideas that we found worked well for us in our fight against the Taiwan Sugar Corporation. We stuck to the facts and gathered as much factual information as we could.

We wish you well. If you need any more information feel free to contact us.

Lisa Phone: (403) 867-2999
Fax: (403) 867-2658
Cell: (403) 647-7887
Email lisab@telusplanet.net

Chapter 8
Bear Hills
by Larry Hubich

For 18 workers from west-central Saskatchewan, getting a job in the big, new hog barn seemed like a lucky break. After all, large-scale hog barn operators claim to bring employment to the rural people who need it most. And they needed it. Most of the workers were under 25, a few married, the rest single. Most of them had lived all their lives on the family farm, or in small towns with few job prospects. For most, this was their first "real" job since graduating high school.

But at the Bear Hills Pork Producers in Biggar and Perdue, Saskatchewan, there were problems from the start. Workers logged 88 hours every two weeks but somehow only got paid for 80. Also, they did not receive premium pay for statutory holidays—including Christmas and New Year's—and sometimes they had to work 11 days at a stretch. Whenever one of the young workers would inquire about overtime or stat-holiday pay, the answer was the same: "You're an agricultural worker, that stuff doesn't apply to you." True. Workers on Canadian farms are not afforded the same kinds of legislated worker benefits that apply in "industrial" jobs.

There were certainly industrial-grade hazards in the hog barn. Workers worried about the heat and the dust, and they had heard about a poisonous gas (hydrogen sulfide) that pig manure gives off. They had even heard about accidents where some workers died after climbing into liquid manure tanks and being overcome by the fumes. But no one knew what to do if a co-worker was to pass out. There was no monitoring or alarm system to warn if gas levels became poisonous. Some workers told me that if they raised these issues they were made to feel like "sucks" or "wimps." It is not macho, in rural Saskatchewan, to raise safety issues.

The bosses did insist that everyone "shower-in" and "shower-out" before entering or leaving the barn. It had to do with bio-security—a concern about humans bringing disease into the barns that would affect the pigs. As more than one young worker told me, "Sometimes they treat the pigs better than us."

My work with the Grain Services Union brought me into contact with these workers in early 1999. On their behalf, I filed an application for union certification of their group with the Saskatchewan Labour Relations Board, which was granted. I then spent nearly a year as part of the bargaining team trying to get a contract from management, something no hog factory workers in Canada, and perhaps North America, had yet done. If that was not enough, the workers also had to fight for recognition from their own government.

Factory Farms and the Law

Large-scale hog barns have been built all over rural North America, despite widespread complaints that they smell bad, pollute the environment, are unsafe to work in, and have poor employment benefits. How do they get away with it?

Hog factories, it seems, are just farms in the eyes of the law in many jurisdictions. Labour standards on farms are less stringent than for "industrial" employers. Minimum standards for statutory holiday pay, overtime rates, worker compensation, and the like do not apply. The same goes for environmental protection, occupational health and safety, and so on.

At least it used to be that way. Things are changing, though hog factory owners are fighting change at every step. Workers of Bear Hills Pork Producers in Saskatchewan discovered that in reality while in the course of becoming the first hog factory union in Canada to negotiate a collective labour contract. Getting the contract took nearly two years and brought the union—and advocates like me—up against both government and the entire pork industry.

In Saskatchewan, employees in the corporate hog industry have been appealing to the government to remove the Labour Standards exemption for hog barn workers since 1997. We have argued that exempting hog barn workers from the basic minimum standards of the Labour Standards Act is unconstitutional and violates the Canadian Charter of Rights and Freedoms.

Courts are beginning to understand that corporate hog factories are not family farms, however much this ruse helps the company bottom line. In 1997 in the state of Kentucky, Attorney General Albert Chandler rendered an opinion that large hog operations are not protected by that state's right-to-farm law. Kentucky defines an "agricultural operation" as one that involves raising livestock or crops "in a reasonable and prudent manner customary among farm operators."

Chandler came to the conclusion that large intensive hog operations are neither reasonable nor prudent when he wrote: " . . . an industrial-scale hog operation with its obligatory lagoon does not qualify in our view as an agricultural resource." He went on to state, "It is rather an industrial operation producing industrial waste."

On July 10, 2002, after five years of delays, the Saskatchewan Legislature passed an amendment to the Labour Standards Act providing that the provisions of the Act will now cover workers in corporate hog operations. The amendment came into effect on September 1, 2002. That means workers in corporate hog factories in Saskatchewan will now be entitled to at least the minimum standards in such areas as (to name a few) hours of work and overtime, periods of

Hog Barn Worker Disease Hazards

Infections
- Erysepeloid (skin infection caused by streptococcus)
- Intestinal infections (caused by Salmonella and Campylobacter)

Upper Airway Disease
- Sinusitis
- Irritant Rhinitis
- Allergic Rhinitis
- Pharyngitis

Lower Airway Disease
- Organic Dust Toxic Syndrome (ODTS)
- Occupational Asthma
- Nonallergic asthma, hyperresponsive airways disease, or reactive airways disease syndrome (RADS)
- Allergic asthma (IgE mediated)
- Acute or Subacute Bronchitis
- Chronic Bronchitis
- Chronic Obstructive Pulmonary Disease

Interstitial Lung Disease
- Alveolitis
- Chronic Interstitial Infiltrate

Hog Barn Worker Injury Hazards

- Eye, nose and throat irritation
- Noise-induced hearing loss
- Hydrogen Sulphide (H2S) poisonings
- Infectious diseases
- Thermal stress
- Tramautic injuries
- Needle sticks
- Carbon Monoxide (CO) poisonings
- Electrocutions
- Drownings

rest, minimum wage, maternity leave, parental leave, annual vacations, and statutory holidays.

During the legislative debates, the industry umbrella organization, Saskatchewan Pork Producers, pushed hard to stop (or at least delay) the amendments. For weeks, SaskPork ran half- and full-page ads twice a week or more in the major daily newspapers proclaiming that the Labour Standards Act would devastate the industry.

Even if that were true—and I do not believe it is—who wants an industry that can not afford the most basic benefits to its workers? Or basic protections to the environment? Intensive hog operations should be required to meet and comply with industrial standards in all legislative areas—labour standards, workers' compensation, occupational health and safety, and of course the environment.

The workers at Bear Hills Pork Producers have shown the way—at least in terms of labour standards in one political jurisdiction. Whether workers elsewhere in the pork industry can force employers to raise their standards remains to be seen.

First Collective Agreement

The tale of the fight for workplace rights at Bear Hills speaks volumes about the hog factory operations that have spread across the continent in recent years. It is also a testament to the workers' resolve. Perhaps food democracy begins where food is produced.

Bear Hills Pork Producers is significantly controlled by Heartland Livestock, in turn a subsidiary of a prairie agricultural giant, the Saskatchewan Wheat Pool. A glance at their colleagues elsewhere in this affluent corporate "family" revealed to the Bear Hills workers that they were being treated as second-class citizens. They knew that workers in the company's grain elevators in the same communities had more rights, labour standards protection, and better benefits.

Unionized or not, the company stuck by its position that hog factory workers were like any other farm labourers, and thus did not fall under the protection of the provincial Labour Standards Act. The Act, which is similar to laws elsewhere in North America, exempts farms from meeting the kinds of basic minimum standards for overtime pay, length of work, rest periods, and so on. Management, it seemed, thought it was running a farm.

There was not one person on the management bargaining team who came from the barn or the local community. All of them were men in suits working out of the head offices of the Pool and Heartland Livestock in Regina. They said that for a "first agreement" and for "the hog industry" what the Bear Hills workers wanted was "too rich." We interpreted such statements to mean that working in the hog industry means poor pay and sub-standard conditions.

The union bargaining team felt as if management was bargaining on behalf of the entire hog factory industry, one that demanded cheap labour. Management refused to include Bear Hills workers in the existing master benefits plan between the Pool (and subsidiaries) and the Grain Services Union. Nor did they want these employees included in the existing pension plan.

There were a number of issues related to how employees would be paid when they worked on statutory holidays. The Bear Hills workers simply wanted to be treated the same as other employees of the Saskatchewan Wheat Pool, but the company was not prepared to budge. The management bargaining team continued to insist that to agree with the union's proposals would put the company at a competitive disadvantage given the "industry standard."

On December 23, 1999, after nearly a year of bargaining frustration, the workers invoked a 40-hour work week, five consecutive 8-hour days from Monday to Friday. No more free overtime, no more free weekends, no more spending Christmas Day in a hog factory instead of at home with the family. That year, management worked on Christmas Day, Boxing Day, and New Year's Day. And then, on Monday, January 3, 2000, the company locked out the workers in an attempt to force them to accept a sub-standard contract.

Management brought in replacement workers. When the workers from Bear Hills learned that some of the scabs were from competitor companies, they again felt as if they were fighting the entire corporate hog industry.

Hog Barn Worker Rights

Occupational Health & Safety

- There are still some jurisdictions where workers classified as Agricultural workers are not covered by OH&S legislation.

Workers' Compensation Benefits

- In many jurisdictions WCB coverage is voluntary for employers who employ workers in this sector. (Including Saskatchewan, and Alberta.)
- In March 2001 the Alberta government's survey results showed the percentage of hog farms (factories) that paid benefits and the type of benefits paid:
  Workers' Compensation 36%
  Accident Insurance 36%
  Health Insurance 13%

Labour/Employment Standards

- Until September of 2002 only British Columbia provided agricultural workers with coverage under the minimum labour standards applicable to most other occupations.
- In November of 2000 the Canadian Federation of Independent Business wrote to the Manitoba Minister of Labour as follows:
  "... 76.3 per cent of CFIB agri-business members are opposed to including intensive livestock operations under such labour standards as limits on hours of work, minimum wage and mandatory pay on extended overtime."

Unionization Rights

- In Canada, at least, a worker's right to unionize in the "agricultural sector" is not specifically prohibited by legislation – except in two provinces – Alberta and Ontario.

Charter/Constitutional Rights

- The Supreme Court of Canada found that the Ontario (Harris) Government's 1995 legislation which excluded agricultural workers from the Ontario Labour Relations Act (right to unionize) was unconstitutional and violated Section 2(d) of the Canadian Charter.

Human Rights

- Many organizations are raising serious questions around the use of "migrant labour" in corporate agri-business due to worker exploitation and suppression of rights under additional repressive legislative exemptions for migrant workers.

During the lockout at Bear Hills, the workers held an open community meeting to discuss the dispute and answer any questions. Everyone was invited, though management refused to attend. In a packed hall in front of friends, family, and interested community folks, the Bear Hills workers defended their position. And the support they received was gratifying.

Close to the end of the evening, the mother of one of the young locked-out workers stood up and said, "Just over a year ago, I was in this very hall and it was the management standing at the front telling us that putting a hog barn in our community was a good thing. They wanted us to invest our money in the barn, and they promised us there would be jobs for our kids. Well, there are jobs all right but without rights they're not good jobs. What else did they tell us that wasn't true?"

After four-and-one-half months walking a picket line, the union applied to the Saskatchewan Labour Relations Board for first agreement mediation, which brought the lockout to an end. The company and the union entered the mediation process and on November 10, 2000, the parties signed a tentative first agreement that the workers felt they could live with.

This first collective agreement, which was ultimately negotiated on the basis of the recommendations of a provincially appointed mediator, had to be enforced by an order of the Saskatchewan Labour Relations Board. In this case they were asked by the union to force the company to live up to what they had agreed to. The Board ordered the agreement into effect in February of 2001 with retroactive wage adjustments going back to February 4 of 1999 (the date of union certification).

This article originally appeared in Synergy Magazine, *issue 11.1.* Synergy, *published in Saskatoon, covers sustainable alternatives in agriculture, food, home-building and more across the prairie bio-region.*

Chapter 9
Down By Law: Two Stories About Using the Law to Stop Intensive Livestock Operations

by Simon Neufeld and Miné Elbi

The Problem of Factory Farms

The livestock industry has expanded tremendously. Hog production has increased by 70% in the last decade alone. Most of this expansion has been the result of farm intensification—producing more animals in less space.

Factory farms are known to have serious environmental and human health implications:

- *They produce too much manure*—In 2001, 164 billion kg of manure was produced. This manure is often spread untreated on nearby land. While we keep the waste, over half of all Canadian hog production is exported to the United States. Canada has become a sewer for our livestock export markets.
- *They cause air pollution*—They are not only responsible for noxious odours, but also toxic gases like hydrogen sulfide and ammonia.
- *They cause drug pollution*—Antibiotics, growth hormones, and other veterinary drugs end up in the animals themselves, and also enter the environment through their manure and urine, contaminating the water, the soil, and our food.
- *They are poorly regulated*—There is no federal oversight, and provincial laws are inconsistent and poorly enforced.
- *Rural residents are at a disadvantage*—Local concerned citizens lack the money, expertise, access, and political clout needed to participate effectively in factory farm decision-making.

Access to Environmental Justice

Although other countries have instituted stricter controls on factory farms to protect the environment, Canadian provincial and federal governments are directly promoting factory farms through subsidies and insufficient regulatory control and enforcement. While governments are fostering the growth of factory farms, citizens are trying to stop them. Opposition takes the form of political lobbying, community protests, petitioning, and legal action.

Citizen groups in rural communities are at an inherent disadvantage when it comes to challenging factory farms, because:

- small communities have less political influence at the provincial and federal levels;
- a smaller population base makes it harder to raise funds to take action;
- legal and scientific expertise is harder to find in rural communities;
- large companies backing factory farms have more resources; and
- provincial legislation does not provide for equitable access to factory farm decision-making.

Founded in 1984, Environmental Defence Canada's mission is to provide Canadians with the tools and knowledge they need to protect and improve their environment and health. We are a national charitable organization committed to engaging the public, finding solutions, and advancing the environmental rights of future generations. We are helping rural groups challenge factory farms across the country, from New Brunswick to Alberta.

The two cases outlined in this chapter highlight groups that we are currently assisting. The focus of a legal challenge varies depending on the legal weaknesses and strengths of the case. Sometimes the weakness of a proposal lies in its environmental impact, such as the potential to contaminate groundwater and thus violate environmental protection laws. Other times, the weakness is procedural, such as when a municipal councilor is in a conflict of interest, which would be dealt with through the laws concerning the responsibilities of elected offices.

The Concerned Daly Ratepayers Inc.

The Concerned Daly Ratepayers Inc. (CDR) is a group of concerned citizens from the municipality of Daly, north of Brandon, Manitoba. The group formed in response to informal plans by Keystone Pig Advancement (KPA) to build an 800-sow hog barn in the municipality. The proposed hog barn was to be built on land designated by the Provincial Water Resource Department as highly susceptible to water contamination. The group was concerned that manure storage lagoons would pose a danger to the municipal drinking water supply.

This case is interesting because the citizen group was able to use political action to achieve a moratorium on all new Intensive Livestock Operations (ILOs) in its municipality. The group wanted the development of stronger by-laws, and is now using the legal system to ensure that the Municipal Council honours these undertakings.

Background

Local residents first heard that the farrow to finish operation was planned for their community in November 2001. The CDR was formed out of the strong community opposition to the proposed operation.

CDR began by circulating a petition to 94% of the community's population calling for a moratorium and stronger by-laws. The petition was signed by 91% of those approached. The strong community support for a moratorium and new by-laws forced the municipality to pass the moratorium as a resolution at the council meeting in February 2002.

The resolution stated that the moratorium would be in place for 90 days, or until new by-laws were developed to govern ILOs. A particularly interesting stand-alone clause of the resolution stated that all new ILO applications would be subject to the new by-laws. This moratorium is at the centre of CDR's legal challenge.

During the Moratorium

CDR was elated that the Council had passed the moratorium. The council had also commissioned CDR to present its concerns in writing. With input from members of the community and with the advice of lawyers, CDR wrote its concerns in the form of by-laws, which were presented to Council and given first reading. A public meeting was scheduled for the following month to discuss the new by-laws.

During the month leading up to the public hearing, several interesting developments occurred. KPA submitted its hog barn application to the municipal council. The application was processed and sent for review to the provincial Technical Review Committee, which is a provincially appointed body that gives recommendations to municipal governments about the technical soundness of ILO proposals.

The Municipal Council also held meetings with its own lawyer and several provincial government staff (including members of the Technical Review Committee) to develop its own set of by-laws. No input from the community was sought during this process. The council's by-laws were released for public review one week before the public meeting.

At the meeting there was overwhelming support for the by-laws submitted by CDR. However, without considering the community's support for the proposed by-laws, Daly Council arbitrarily nullified the moratorium, ended the by-law amendment process, and began consideration of the KPA application under the old by-laws. A date for the KPA Conditional Use Hearing was set for the following month. Manitoba municipalities are required to hold Conditional Use Hearings for all ILO proposals over 400 animal units.

The Legal Challenge

CDR's legal case is built on the fact that the Council has not honoured its resolution to pass new by-laws to control ILOs. It argues that Daly Council's resolution to cancel the moratorium and proceed with the KPA application was made in bad faith. A resolution can be declared invalid under the *Municipal Act* if it was made in bad faith.

CDR also applied for an injunction on KPA's Conditional Use Hearing until the case was decided. However, CDR lost the injunction and the hearing proceeded despite the ongoing legal process.

At the hearing there was tremendous pressure from the community—almost every presentation at the hearing was against the operation. After 16 hours of presentations, Daly Municipal Council rejected the KPA application. The fact that KPA's engineering firm had failed to inform the council that its manure storage plan had been rejected by Manitoba Conservation did not help KPA's case.

CDR still plans to follow through with its legal challenge to have new by-laws put in place. The group is also filing an official complaint to the Association of Professional Engineers and Geoscientists of Manitoba regarding the practices of KPA's engineering firm.

Committee for Lone Pine

Alberta passed a new law in January 2002 that effectively removed factory farm decision-making power from municipalities and put it in the hands of the provincial government. The same government that is actively promoting factory farms is taking control over their approval. The legislation, called the *Agricultural Operation Practices Act,* gives the Natural Resources Conservation Board (NRCB) jurisdiction over factory farm permits.

The Committee for Lone Pine (CLP) was formed in response to an application by AAA Cattle Company to expand a cattle feedlot from 2,500 to 17,000 animals. The application process began before the passing of the *Agricultural Operation Practices Act*, and continues now that the legislation has passed.

The Natural Resources Conservation Board

The NRCB is an independent, quasi-judicial agency reporting to the Minister of Sustainable Development. It was given the responsibility to regulate Confined Feeding Operations in January 2002. The mandate of the NRCB with relation to factory farms is to "determine whether these projects are in the public interest, which means balancing the social, environmental and economic interests of Albertans" (NRCB, 2002). When a producer or a company wants to build a new livestock operation, or expand its feedlot to accommodate more animals, it now applies to the NRCB instead of the local municipality.

Prior to the Agricultural Operation Practices Act

AAA Cattle Company first began stocking its feedlot in Didsbury in the summer of 1999, having applied for a permit to feed 2,500-5,000 animals. The County of Mountain View believed the water supply could support no more than 2,500 head and issued a permit within those parameters. In December 2000, when the permit was finally issued for a maximum of 2,500 animals, there were already more than 7,000 head of cattle on site.

In October 2001, AAA applied to the Alberta Ministry of the Environment to increase the feedlot's water-taking permit from 39,000 gallons per day to 134,000 gallons. Local community members heard of the application and alerted the County of Lone Pine to the fact that AAA was violating its permit. The Committee for Lone Pine was formed to put greater pressure on the County to keep the feedlot limited to 2,500 animals.

In December 2001, the Mountain View Municipal Planning Division, the planning authority under the jurisdiction of the county, gave AAA until July 2002 to comply with its permit. The company was not to bring in any new cattle to the feedlot until the number of animals dropped to the permitted level.

Following implementation of the Agricultural Operation Practices Act

When the Agricultural Operation Practices Act came into effect in January 2002, the Mountain View Municipal Planning Division turned over the enforcement of AAA's permit to the NRCB. Interestingly, while the NRCB was investigating the non-compliance of AAA's permit, it received an application from AAA for an expanded feedlot. However, the NRCB did not begin processing the application until it had completed its investigation of the permit violation.

As a result of its investigation, the NRCB issued an enforcement order on March 21, 2002 stating that AAA must comply with its permit. The NRCB gave AAA until the end of August to reduce its numbers to 2,500, and continued to allow new cattle to be brought on site. The enforcement order would be cancelled if AAA's expansion application were approved by the NRCB.

The differences in enforcement under the old and the new authorities are striking:

- Where the Mountain View Planning Division had given AAA until July to comply with its permit, the NRCB gave AAA until the end of August—almost two months longer.
- Where the local government would not allow new cattle to be added to the herd until compliance was reached, the NRCB allowed new cattle to be added to the herd without compliance.
- The NRCB began reviewing AAA's application for an expanded feedlot in spite of the fact that the feedlot was in violation of its permit.

On August 24, 2002, AAA requested that the deadline to reduce its numbers be extended from August 31 to October 31, 2002. The rationale was that this added time would allow the NRCB review officer to complete the review of AAA's application to expand. The NRCB granted this request.

The Committee for Lone Pine's participation

The Committee for Lone Pine had been involved in much of this regulatory process, making submissions to the Alberta Ministry of

Environment about the water-taking issue and trying to participate in the NRCB review. However, the Committee's access to the decision-making process was severely restricted in several ways.

The NRCB requires that any party not directly adjacent to a proposed livestock operation must apply to be considered an "affected party." Only affected parties are allowed to participate and it is up to the discretion of the NRCB to decide who will be recognized. The Committee for Lone Pine was not granted affected party status, and was forced to participate indirectly through local community members who were granted status. In addition, the community was given only 30 days to review AAA's application, apply for affected party status, and submit comments to the NRCB.

Despite this restriction on public participation, the Committee has been able to participate by hiring a lawyer to help with the written submissions and a hydrogeologist to critique the application.

The NRCB denied the expansion application on November 7, 2002. The application was rejected due to insufficient information about the manure storage facility. AAA plans to resubmit its application once the necessary information has been collected. The Committee for Lone Pine will be there to support the community's opposition.

Conclusions

Taking legal action to stop a factory farm can be expensive, time consuming, and divisive. Yet the only option left for community groups after open discussion and political action has failed is to let the courts decide.

The legal system must support the efforts of rural community members to protect their environment and their health. Environmental Defence Canada calls on the federal government to take a leadership position on this issue. It must institute a moratorium on factory farms until:

- environmental and human health concerns have been addressed;
- an open and transparent approval process for factory farms has been established; and

- citizens have access to the financial and technical resources they need to effectively participate in decisions about factory farms in their communities.

References

NRCB. (2002). *Building a regulatory framework*. Edmonton: Government of Alberta publication, [On-line] at http://www.nrcb.gov.ab.ca/regframewrk.pdf.

Chapter 10
Beyond Our Own Backyards: Factory Farming and the Political Economy of Extraction

by Roger Epp

A Crash Course in Globalization

Organized local opposition to factory hog-barn developments is one of the most significant recent signs of political life in rural Canada. Though it is still all-too-easily dismissed as a "variant of the NIMBY syndrome" (Yakabuski, 2002), such not-in-my-backyard caricatures are disturbing. They imply that the responsibility for the world exercised in one's own neighbourhood is dishonourable and that rural people should instead willingly accept developments that risk their health, livelihood, quality of life, and property values for the sake of provincial economic strategies and corporate profits.

Second, the NIMBY brush-off misrepresents the growing self-understanding of opposition groups and the coalitions they have begun to form. Over and over, the fight to keep a large hog-barn complex out of the neighbourhood has become much more. It does not end if the developers are forced to find a new site downriver, downwind, or in the next municipality. Ultimately it is not really a fight *against* anything. Rather, this movement, sparked by intense promotion of the hog industry from New Brunswick to Alberta, makes sense and can only be sustained insofar as it represents a positive vision of its own.

That vision is about a different countryside than the one that governments and corporate investors apparently have in mind. It is about a different rural economy—less extractive, more resilient, and more respectful of people's livelihoods, local knowledge, and environmental limits. It is about a different food system—more decentralized, and therefore safer and more sustainable, than the continental and global one that is being shaped by a small cluster of vertically-integrated processing giants. And, not least, it is about a different democratic politics in which real authority is restored to communities. The stakes are that high, and they unite rural people in Canada with those in North Carolina and Iowa, Mexico and Poland.

That is the core argument of this chapter. There is nothing easy, all the same, about what amounts to a crash-course, first-hand education in the political economy of globalization, whose effects arguably are most visible in rural communities (see Epp & Whitson, 2001; Qualman & Wiebe, 2002). Family farms operate with diminished market power, caught in a relentless cost-price squeeze. While there *is* still plenty of money being made from agriculture, less of it is returned to primary producers or stays in local circulation. Statistics Canada's labour-force survey shows a dramatic decline in the number of people across the country who identify themselves as engaged primarily in farming: as many as 40% in Alberta and 36% in Saskatchewan between 1998 and 2001 (Wilson, 2002).

Provincial governments that once built rural infrastructures and took other steps to ensure the long-term health of farm-based communities have put on a very different face. Their interest in agriculture is less about producers than it is about the production of "raw materials" that cheaply and reliably available, will entice food-and-fibre processors to locate in their province rather than somewhere else. Governments' role generally is to package provinces competitively for investment ("to create jobs"). It is not to defend vital sectors of the economy like food production or to balance opportunities across a whole society. Accordingly, urban-rural disparities have widened, strikingly so in places like Alberta, where they are masked by province-wide growth figures and by a mythology of prosperity that is hard to challenge (Government of Alberta, 2002; MacArthur, 2002).

Rural people commonly use the language of abandonment. They feel they are on their own in defending their communities. Some of them are tired from struggles to save schools, hospitals, rail-lines, post offices, and their own farms, or from spreading volunteer energies too thinly to keep churches, hockey teams, and cultural activities alive. They have watched friends move away. And then they hear—they may or may not be properly notified—that land is being assembled, that neighbours have been approached for permission to spread manure, and that an application has been submitted for a development permit to build a 5,000 or 6,000 or 7,000-sow barn complex. Their provincial government may have recruited the applicant company, or may even own an equity share in it, as in Saskatchewan with Big Sky Pork. The province may have supplied a manual on how to set up an intensive livestock operation, including topics such as how to minimize local opposition by avoiding public meetings and isolating the "troublemakers" in the community. The province may have helped with site selection.

This scenario is familiar enough, if still bewildering, to people who assume that governments at least should protect the interests of citizens. What becomes obvious when the gaze of political experience is redirected beyond any particular backyard is the similarity among stories, the government policy shifts, and sometimes the company names. But what else comes into view? What assumptions? What configurations of political and economic power? What proof that governments and communities do have choices? What serious thinking is prompted as part of the work of defending rural communities and exercising local responsibility for that same world?

The Farm of the 21st Century

The first image—literally—that I want to consider is a picture that accompanied an article in *National Geographic* magazine in 1970 on *The Revolution in American Agriculture* (Billard, 1970). Drawn under the advisement of agronomists with the United States Department of Agriculture, at the time when governments first told farmers to "get big or get out," the picture is a reminder that the dream of industrial-scale farming has been around a long time. Indeed, as James Scott describes in great detail, million-acre corporate-owned farms in places like Montana in the first quarter of the 20th century—farms

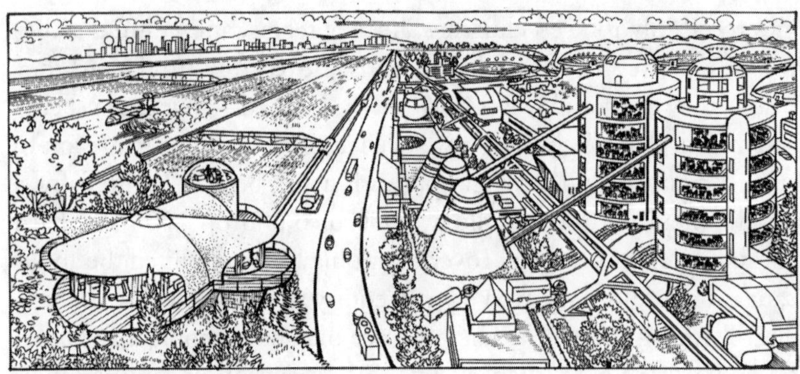
D. Geary after David Meltzer N.G.S. 1970

whose main advantage was not "efficiency" but preferred status with lawmakers and banks—may have been less resilient than family farms, but they looked like the future to agronomists. At the onset of collectivization, they also attracted favourable notice in the Soviet Union, which tried to lure corporate managers to its own bold experiments in agriculture. The Soviets were more successful in enlisting American agronomists who, working for handsome fees in Chicago hotel rooms, planned collective farms for places and climates they would never see—down to the details of crop rotations and inputs (Scott, 1998).

The picture in *National Geographic* betrays the same boundless faith in expert knowledge and efficiencies of scale, reassuringly projected into the early 21st century. The farmhouse is a bubble-topped, Jetson's-style "control tower" overlooking a stunningly clean, powerful vista. Harvesting and other equipment glide on tracks over ten-mile-long grain-fields. High-rise cattle feedlots are linked onsite to conical feed-mills and to a processing plant that packs beef for shipment to market by monorail, while, according to the caption, "a tubular side drain flushes wastes to be broken down for fertilizer." Certainly there is no manure in the picture. There are no farmers either, and no visible marks of rural community, such as a school bus. It is not clear who owns this farm, or who could afford to own it, given its size and capital requirements.

Industry and Government

There are no farms on the Canadian prairies like the one portrayed in the picture, though it might be said that considerable progress has been made towards the half-way step of depleting the countryside of small, mixed, independent producers. The consolidation of the hog sector in particular has been dramatic and relatively recent across North America. The downturn in pork prices in the fall of 2002 will complete it, while the largest commercial producers—led by Smithfield Foods at 700,000 sows—will make their profit on the processing side of their operations (Qualman, 2001; Heffernan, 1999). As an Alberta government publication, *Bacon Bits* (1999), coolly advised its readers, independent producers would be no more than a "residual supply group" in the "New Agriculture."

When you look beyond your own backyard, it is hard not to notice that the hog industry is now highly concentrated, vertically integrated, mobile, and, for now, continental in its organization. The top five pork packers in the U.S. [Smithfield, Tyson, ConAgra (Swift), Cargill (Excel), and Farmland] account for at least 75% of all processing in that country (Heffernan & Hendrickson, 2002). The same companies are among the largest commercial producers of hogs. They are also the top five in beef, with an even larger combined share of processing, and they have made serious inroads into Canada by various means, including direct purchase (Smithfield, for example, now owns Schneiders and, as of November 2002, Mitchells in Saskatoon). If the consolidation and factory-style expansion of hog production began in the U.S., in places like North Carolina where it was encouraged as a high-value substitute for tobacco (e.g., Stull & Broadway, 2003; Foruseth, 2001; Thu & Durrenberger, 1998), the industry is now spreading far beyond those borders. Indeed, it faces some serious new challenges inside the U.S.: a moratorium in North Carolina; strict environmental and animal-welfare regulation in some states, including a constitutional ban approved by Florida voters in November 2002 on the crating of pregnant sows; jury awards such as the $33 million against Iowa Select Farms in October 2002 to complainants living near its barns; and attempts in some states to limit packing plants' ownership of livestock.

As the pendulum swings from promotion to prosecution, it is no surprise that the biggest players are looking to Eastern Europe; to Mexico, where more employees at lower wages can reduce mortality rates in the barns (see Freese, 2001); and, of course, to Canada, where provincial governments have aggressively promoted the industry—in the West as a post-Crow substitute for a hard-hit export-grain economy—and where outside capital will be required to achieve anything near politicians' higher and higher production targets of at least 10 million hogs in some provinces. Their efforts were helped by the U.S.-based industry magazine, *Successful Farming* (Freese, 2000), which reported that "[w]hile the big boys down here sit on their hands, stymied by a myriad of new laws and regulations, the Canadians are dreaming big." Indeed. There are now more pigs than people across the three prairie provinces (Statistics Canada, 2001); and if that is a surprise, it is a measure of isolation from the contemporary realities of food production and rural life.

Governments, in turn, must be understood not simply as having promoted the expansion of hog production, but as having promoted a certain kind of industry. Among other things, at a provincial level, they have eliminated single-desk selling agencies, to the distinct disadvantage of small producers. They have extended loan guarantees and other forms of financial assistance to corporate producers. Typically, they have declared factory hog barns to be "farms" and therefore exempt from industrial labour standards. Whether incrementally or decisively, as in Alberta, they have eroded municipal decision-making authority over intensive-livestock or confined feeding operations, in order to ensure that neither local objectors nor upstart councils can stop "science-based" developments or harm provincial reputations as safe havens for agri-business investment. On top of all this, they have propagated the kind of verbal violence implied in ritual catch-phrases like "value-added," which might be re-interpreted in this context to mean that it is industrial processing that creates wealth and that farmers at the bottom of the value-chain should be satisfied to grow feed grain and sell it to the nearest ILO at prices competitive with subsidized U.S. corn or cheap-currency Ukrainian barley.

There was predictable outrage in provincial capitals, in the spring of 2002, when the *Ottawa Citizen* obtained internal Agriculture Canada documents suggesting that governments were promoting the "good news" of intensive hog production in the face of evidence about significant health and environmental problems. Not that the federal government had any plans to press for a change in direction. According to the same story, Agriculture Canada's communications strategy was to "reduce public resistance to hog operations by education and by showing that the economic benefits of a thriving pork industry can be achieved without compromising the environment or rural quality of life." In other words, the problem lay in the domain of public relations (Spears, 2002).

It would be possible to account for the rise of factory hog production in Canada with a purely political-economic analysis, stressing the role of corporate power in a global economy that reduces provinces and municipalities to the role of anxious supplicants. But that analysis would be incomplete no matter how much evidence it cites. Part of what family farm people face, and what makes their landscapes the target of industrialization, is a cultural shift in a society that is increasingly urban and disconnected from the working countryside. They are no longer romanticized as the backbone of the country. Far from it. Economists and politicians tell them to move where the jobs are. National newspaper columnists routinely decry farm "subsidies" and foresee the end of farming; or else they accuse parents who raise children in rural communities as guilty of something akin to abuse for depriving them of the big-city educational and cultural opportunities that will be crucial to their individual career prospects. As the writer Andrew Nikiforuk has put it, rural people are "becoming an endangered species as well as an abused one" (personal interview, 2002).

Increasingly, rural people may also be in the way. From the perspective of governments and outside investors, the countryside is no longer understood in terms of rooted human settlement and livelihood. Rather, it is coming to serve two very different purposes. The prettiest places become up-scale playgrounds: tourist resorts, golf courses, parks, or weekend property with a view of the mountains. The rest—mostly out of sight, out of mind—are envisioned as either resource plantations or dumping grounds. They are "empty."

The real desperation in rural communities where populations have declined and economic prospects seem limited ensures that even the most divisive, dubious, and messy development will find local support. This is the new spatial division of labour in the global economy. It means increasingly that family-farm agriculture has become a tolerated land-use, so long as it does not interfere with preferred and presumably more productive industrial uses: petroleum, pulp, power generation, and now pigs—all of them large-scale, export-oriented, and water-consuming. The clear message to rural people, delivered at "stakeholder" conferences with Orwellian titles (*The Land Supports Us All*), is that they will have to move over—and share the water. It is no exaggeration to say it is open season on the rural environment, on family-farm producers, and on local democracy.

Listening to Americans

There is a self-satisfied myopia among Canadians when it comes to looking south beyond their own backyards and learning from American experience and practice. To be sure, there are fringe organizations committed to making Canada—at least Alberta—the 51st state; their members imagine a paradise of swashbuckling free enterprise. The real U.S., however, is filled with lessons about possible political and legal responses, some listed above, to factory hog operations.

The real U.S. even includes states like Nebraska and South Dakota, whose constitutions have been amended by popular initiative to prohibit corporations from owning farmland or operating farms. While the Nebraska amendment has been subject to exceptions and uneven enforcement since it was passed in 1982, an active citizens group remains vigilant in its defence; the state's attorney-general successfully filed suit against Seaboard Farms in 2000 for violating the ban through a third-party arrangement with other pork producers (CFRA, 2001). In South Dakota, the amendment passed in 1998 specifically excludes hog confinement facilities. In language that is inconceivable in Canadian federal or provincial statutes, its general preamble recognizes both "the importance of the family farm to the economic and moral stability of the state" and the threat to it posed by "conglomerates" (State of South Dakota, n.d.).

The South Dakota amendment has been subject to persistent political and legal challenge, partly on behalf of intensive-livestock operators; and a U.S. District Court judge did rule in spring 2002 that it failed to meet constitutional requirements having to do with utility easements and the rights of the disabled (though he upheld the state's authority to restrict corporate ownership). Nonetheless, the provision continues to enjoy popular support. The state will appeal the court ruling. And, in the meantime, voters have rejected an amendment that was perceived to soften the prohibition (CFRA, 2002).

The real U.S. that rural people in Canada would do well to know includes sites of useful, sympathetic research: among them, the Center for Rural Affairs (Nebraska), the Columbia Food Circle based at the University of Missouri, the Land Institute (Kansas), and the Institute for Agriculture and Trade Policy (Minnesota). It includes working alliances between rural people and environmental groups like the Sierra Club (U.S.)or Waterkeepers, and social justice organizations like the National Catholic Rural Life Conference. It includes broad-based activist organizations like Dakota Rural Action or the Northern Plains Research Council, part of a network of state-level organizations concerned with family farms, main-street business, soil and groundwater resources, air quality, and responsible regulation of energy and mining developments—precisely against the prospect of an industrialized, depopulated countryside that can be treated as a dumping ground or resource plantation by outside investors.

Conclusion

In a global economy characterized by transience, the most radical counter-position is to be found in living out a commitment to a particular place and its well-being. In rural communities threatened by factory hog operations, the effort to keep them out represents a deeper, instinctive preference for a different countryside, a different rural economy, a different food system, a different relation to land and livestock, and a different, democratic politics (see Regier, 2002). It represents a turning point in which people overcome the temptation to personalize the threat of a factory hog-barn in an arrogant municipal councillor or an opportunistic local landowner. It represents a turning point in which rural people—smart, articulate, cantankerous, too aloof from politics for too long—begin to realize how much they are on their own, how they need to organize to defend their community interests, and how, in the end, they find that they share interests with many other people across a whole continent. Sometimes the ad hoc groups they form are unpolished and angry. Often it is women who emerge as leaders.

The effort is a demanding one. It is filled with steep learning curves and the discomfort of unresolved political conflict in face-to-face rural communities. It takes organization and coalition-building. It takes money for legal bills. It takes quick expertise in science and regulatory processes. It takes political skills: speaking on behalf of a group, listening, making decisions, and making sense of what experience teaches about the location and nature of power.

More than that, it is an effort that takes thinking-through: What about family farms and rural communities is worth conserving? How to put into words what rural people know instinctively to be true? Surely one of those things is that the most sustainable economy and community is one in which ownership is widely dispersed, not concentrated. Another is that decisions vital to that community belong, in large measure, with those who must live with their consequences. Democracy requires nothing less.

References

Billard, J. (1970, February). The revolution in American agriculture. *National Geographic, 137*, 147-85.

Center for Rural Affairs (CFRA). (2001, November). Corporate farming notes. *Newsletter*, p. 3.

Center for Rural Affairs (CFRA). (2002, July). Amendment A fails in South Dakota. *Newsletter*, p. 4.

Epp, R., & Whitson, D. (Eds.). (2001). *Writing off the rural west: Globalization, governments, and the transformation of rural communities*. Edmonton: University of Alberta Press/Parkland Institute.

Foruseth, O. (2001, May). Hog farming in eastern North Carolina. *Southeastern Geographer, 41*, 53-64.

Freese, B. (2000, October). Sow herd building again: This time it's Canada making the move. *Successful Farming*.

Freese, B. (2001, September). Making moves in Mexico. *Successful Farming*.

Government of Alberta. Agriculture, Food, and Rural Development. (1999, December). The aftermath of the crisis: Rethinking the chain approach. *Bacon Bits, 12*.

Government of Alberta, Economic Development. (2002, March 4). *Regional Disparities in Alberta: Resource Package*.

Heffernan, William. (1999). *Consolidation in the food and agriculture system*. Report to the National Farmers Union (U.S.).

Heffernan, W., & Hendrickson, H. (2002). *Multi-national concentrated food processing and marketing systems and the farm crisis*. Paper presented at the annual meeting of the American Association for the Advancement of Science Symposium: Science and Sustainability. Boston.

MacArthur, M. (2002, May 30). Report tells tale of two Albertas. *Western Producer*, p. 1.

Qualman, D. (2001). Corporate hog farming. In R. Epp and D. Whitson(Eds.), *Writing off the rural west: Globalization, governments, and the transformation of rural communities* (pp. 21-38). Edmonton: University of Alberta Press/Parkland Institute.

Qualman, D., & Wiebe, N. (2002). *The structural adjustment of Canadian agriculture*. Ottawa: Canadian Centre for Policy Alternatives.

Regier, Elaine. (2002, June 13). Family farm suffers yet another drastic blow. *Saskatoon Star-Phoenix.*

Scott, J. (1998). *Seeing like a state.* New Haven: Yale University Press.

Spears, T. (2002, March 19). Health fears mount over industrial hog farms. *Edmonton Journal*, pp. A1-2.

State of South Dakota. (n.d.). *Constitution.* Article 17.21. [On-line]. Available: http://legis.state.sd.us/statutes/index.

Statistics Canada. (2001). *Census of Agriculture.* Livestock by provinces. [On-line]. Available: http://www.statcan.ca/english/Pgdb/census.htm.

Stull, D., & Broadway, M. (2003). *Slaughterhouse blues: The meat and poultry industry in North America.* Belmont, CA: Wadsworth.

Thu, K., & Durrenberger, P. (Eds.). (1998). *Pigs, profits, and rural communities.* Albany: State University of New York Press.

Wilson, B. (2002, February 28). Farm job totals shrink. *Western Producer*, p. 1.

Yakabuski, K. (2002, September). High on the hog. *Report on Business Magazine*, pp. 61-69.

Suggested Reading and Viewing

Books

Epp, R., & Whitson, D. (Eds.). (2001). *Writing off the rural west: Globalization, governments, and the transformation of rural communities*. Edmonton: University of Alberta Press and Parkland Institute.

Kimbrell, A. (Ed.). (2002). *Fatal harvest: The tragedy of industrial agriculture.* Washington: Island Press.

Korten, D. (1995). *When corporations rule the world.* San Francisco: Berret-Koehler Publishers, Inc.

Magdoff, F., Bellamy Foster, J., & Buttel, F. (Eds.). (2000). *Hungry for profit: The agribusiness threat to farmers, food, and the environment*. New York: Monthly Review Press.

Roberts, W., MacRae, R., & Stahlbrand, L. (Eds.). (1999). *Real food for change: Bringing nature, health, joy, and justice to the table*. Toronto: Random House of Canada.

Schlosser, E. (2002). *Fast food nation: The dark side of the all-American meal.* New York: Perennial.

Stull, D., & Broadway, M. (2003). *Slaughterhouse Blues: The meat and poultry industry in North America.* Belmont, CA: Wadsworth.

Thu, K., & Durrenberger, P. (Eds.). (1998). *Pigs, profits, and rural communities*. Albany: State University of New York Press.

Videos

Bacon: The Film. (2001). Montreal: National Film Board of Canada.

And on this Farm. (1998). Burnsville MN: Field Pictures.

About the Contributors, Editors, and Cover Artist

Contributors

Lisa Bechthold lives on a 3rd generation farm in Southern Alberta. She became involved when the Taiwanese Sugar Corporation proposed a 7,200-sow farrow-to-finish hog operation near her farm. The proposal was successfully defeated. Lisa joined the GRACE Factory Farm Project team in February 2001 and works with groups across Canada who need help in dealing with factory farm issues. She is one of the founders and Vice-President of Alberta's Society for Environmentally Responsible Livestock Operations (SERLO), which was formed in April 2002. Lisa is on the steering committee for the Beyond Factory Farming Coalition.

Rick Dove is Southeastern Representative for the Waterkeeper Alliance in North Carolina, lawyer, commercial fisher, and writer whose most recent work is a chapter in the book *And the Water Turned to Blood.* He works relentlessly at warning other communities of the dangers of hog mega-barns by sharing the North Carolina experience, which has been devastating.

Miné Elbi was a Communications Officer at Environmental Defence Canada. She has a Bachelor of Science from Ryerson University in Toronto and has recently completed her post-graduate certificate in Corporate Communications from Seneca College. Before joining Environmental Defence Canada, Miné was a technical support and customer liaison officer at Vector Biosystems.

Roger Epp is Professor of Political Studies and Interim Academic Dean at Augustana University College in Camrose, Alberta. He is co-editor of the book *Writing Off the Rural West (2001)*, to which he also contributed a chapter on the political "deskilling" of rural communities. Roger is a frequent speaker and media commentator on rural political and land-use issues. His current research and writing is focused on agrarian ideas and political movements. Roger is a founding member of the Kingman Renaissance Research Institute, a lively weekly forum on public affairs.

Larry Hubich is the President of the Saskatchewan Federation of Labour. He was a staff representative with the Grain Services Union for 20 years and a member since 1973.

John Ikerd is Professor Emeritus of Agricultural Economics. He was raised on a small dairy farm in southwest Missouri and received his BS, MS, and Ph.D. degrees from the University of Missouri. John worked in private industry for a time and spent 30 years in various professorial positions at four major Land Grant universities before retiring from the University of Missouri in early 2000. Since retiring, John spends most of his time writing and speaking on issues related to the sustainability of agriculture.

Simon Neufeld, as a researcher at Environmental Defence Canada, led the organization's work on food safety under the FoodWatch program. He has completed a Bachelor of Science in Agroecology, focusing on the interaction between agriculture and the social, political, and ecological environment in which it takes place. Simon has worked as a graduation gown shipping assistant, a camp instructor, researcher for the University of Manitoba and Agriculture and Agri-food Canada, and as a research and planning coordinator for the Canadian Wheat Board. His research interests include rural community development, sustainable agriculture, and globalization.

Bill Paton, born in Kilwinning, Scotland, is a biologist and the coordinator of the Agricultural Program at the University of Brandon. His research interests include: tree decline, alternative energy, solid waste management/composting, pollution biology, and horticulture. Bill's most recent publication is *The Hudson Bay Drainage System: Conflicts and Cooperation in Transboundary Water Quantity and Quality*. He frequently appears as a speaker at water-related forums. Bill is a member of the Technical Advisory committee to design a wastewater treatment facility for the City of Brandon and a member of the Manitoba Hazardous Waste Corporation.

Brian Storey is a high school teacher living in Ontario and the chair of Hogwatch Haldimand. Offended by the environmental policies of the Harris/Eves government, he has become active in provincial Liberal organizing and is co-chair of the local campaign for the up-coming election. He sees cartoons, poems, and songs such as the one in this volume as a form of art therapy, more than art itself.

Fred Tait farms in Rossendale, Manitoba with his wife, Sandra. He was Vice President of the National Farmers Union from December 1998 to December 2002 and also served as Regional Coordinator from 1991-98. Fred is the President of Hog Watch Manitoba which under the leadership team has become a leading North American organization in opposing vertically-integrated, factory farm production of hogs. Fred is a member of the Manitoba Office of the Canadian Centre for Policy Alternatives.

Kendall Thu is an Associate Professor in the Department of Anthropology at Northern Illinois University. He chairs the Committee on Public Policy for the American Anthropological Association, is a Fellow in the Society for Applied Anthropology, and serves on the Executive Committee of the Central States Anthropological Society. Kendall's current research focuses on industrial food systems. He has published a range of articles on the rapid industrialization of the livestock sector, including one in *Pigs, Profits, and Rural Communities,* a book that he co-edited. Kendall has also written several scientific and popular articles on the community and health dimensions of industrialized agriculture.

Bill Weida is Director of the GRACE Factory Farm Project. He recently retired as Professor of Economics and Business at The Colorado College where he specialized in regional economics, statistics, and econometric modeling. Bill received a BS in engineering from the U.S. Air Force Academy, an MBA from UCLA, and a Doctorate in Econometrics and Operations Research from the University of Colorado. He has published a large number of articles, written four books, and contributed chapters to four others—all of which deal with the regional economic impact of large projects. Bill has spent the last 15 years providing advice to communities and regions on the impacts of various forms of economic development.

Editors

Alexander (Sandy) Ervin is Professor of Anthropology at the University of Saskatchewan. His specialties include applied medical and environmental anthropology and the study of sociocultural change and globalization. Sandy is the author and co-author of three books including *Applied Anthropology: Tools and Perspectives for Contemporary Practice*, as well as about forty articles and technical reports in applied anthropology. A board member of the Saskatchewan Office of the Canadian Centre for Policy Alternatives, he is also active in local peace, environmental, and social justice issues, and The Sierra Club of Canada.

Cathy Holtslander was Coordinator of the Saskatchewan Eco Network from 1997 to 2003, and is currently the Council of Canadians' national organizer on the factory farming issue. She studied the Saskatchewan farm/co-operative movement of the 1920s and 1930s, focusing on the leadership of women, for her Masters in Adult and Continuing Education. Cathy has published a few academic articles, but has been most interested in writing for a general audience. She co-published and edited *Synergy* magazine in the 1990s and has written many articles about organic agriculture and various environmental issues. Cathy is also on the Board of CCPA-Saskatchewan.

Darrin Qualman has lived and farmed most of his life at Dundurn, Saskatchewan. He stopped farming in 2000. He worked on energy and environmental issues in the early 1990s and became the Executive Secretary of the National Farmers Union in June of 1996, a position he still holds. Darrin is the author of an influential report entitled: *The Farm Crisis, EU Subsidies, and Agri-Business Market Power* that places the blame for the farm income crisis squarely on corporate power and profiteering. He has made presentations on agricultural and trade issues across Canada and in Europe and is currently working on a report on the extractive nature of the global corporate economy.

Rick Sawa is the Director of the Saskatchewan Office of the Canadian Centre of Policy Alternatives. He is also a doctoral candidate in Educational Administration at the University of Saskatchewan and the title of his dissertation is: *More Responsive to and Diverse for Whom?: The Perceived Effects on Three Public Schools of a Charter School in Calgary, Alberta.* Rick is a long-time educator who has presented on the following educational topics: charter schools, education and globalization, teacher evaluation policy, and school discipline. He is a founding member of the Prince Albert Chapter of the Council of Canadians.

Cover Artist

Dave Geary earned a Bachelor of Fine Arts and a Masters of Fine Arts from the University of Saskatchewan. He is an artist, illustrator, and writer living in Saskatoon and works for an educational publishing company. Dave has a strong interest in natural sciences and environmental issues.